ALL ABOUT
ANIMALS

Written by Rebecca Taylor

**NURSERY
WORLD**

TES
THE TIMES EDUCATIONAL SUPPLEMENT

NURSERY WORLD

TES
THE TIMES EDUCATIONAL SUPPLEMENT

Managing Editor Patricia Grogan
Art Editor Clare Shedden

Photography Andy Crawford

Editor Samantha Gray
Editorial assistant Edward FitzGerald
Consultant Marian Whitehead

First published in Great Britain in 1999 by
Times Supplements Limited
Admiral House, 66–68 East Smithfield, London E1 9XY

A CIP catalogue record for this book is available
from the British Library

ISBN 1-84122-003-5

Colour reproduction by Prima Creative Services, UK
Printed and bound in Belgium by Proost

Nursery World would like to thank the children
and staff at the following Nurseryworks nurseries
for taking part in this book:
Jigsaw Day Nursery, Stevenage,
Jigsaw Day Nursery, Welwyn Garden City

CONTENTS

INTRODUCTION

All **About Animals** contains more than 100 activities divided into seven chapters. Each chapter explores one avenue of the book's central theme. The activities are self-contained but also build on from each other, so you can dip into several chapters when planning your theme or you can use complete chapters. All the activities are firmly underpinned by seven areas of learning to help you incorporate them into your planning. The topic web on pages 10–11 shows you into which areas of learning each activity falls and each activity has symbols representing the areas of learning covered.

Planning a curriculum

The activities in this book are suitable for curriculum planning to follow all the early years guidelines across the United Kingdom. It is now widely accepted that nursery-age children learn best through play, and it is essential to include child-led play when planning a curriculum. Many of the activities on the following pages also give extension ideas to promote this kind of learning. However, the book should not be seen as a complete curriculum – its purpose is to help you put together an educationally balanced, varied and exciting curriculum for nursery-age children. Each activity covers one or more of the following areas of learning: Personal and Social Development, Language and Literacy, Mathematical Development, Science and Technology, Time and Place, Physical Development and Creative Development.

Personal and Social Development

This area of learning should be given the greatest emphasis in a nursery curriculum, so many of the activities focus on the children working individually and as part of a group in a constructive way. The nursery is the stage in all children's lives when they learn how to communicate appropriately with others outside their immediate family. There are activities to teach them about sharing, taking turns, showing interest in and playing with other children, making friends, accepting guidance and direction from adults, concentrating and completing tasks, as well as learning how to dress and undress independently and remove and put on shoes. When the children are used to the nursery routine and to one another, and trust that the adults they see at nursery are consistent, positive and encouraging, they will feel confident enough to continue to develop personally and socially.

Language and Literacy

In this area of learning, children develop their speaking and listening skills and literacy. The activities encourage them to respond to stories, rhymes and poems, look at a variety of books, read books to themselves and others, make up stories, attempt to write, write their own names, write some familiar letters and words, know some different letter sounds and understand that writing has different purposes. Listening to children talk is a crucial element of developing language and literacy. Nursery children are not generally fluent writers but communicate best through speech and gesture. Verbal praise and eye contact encourage children to talk and reveal more about their knowledge and understanding. By reading and writing stories, children can be transported to different places and have imaginary adventures. They discover these imaginative places by reading, and create them for themselves by writing. The first step children take towards learning to write is making marks with paint and chalk. Several activities in this book give children opportunities to experiment independently with writing as well as to participate in collaborative writing with an adult acting as scribe so that they can start to communicate by writing. There are also creative and physical activities to develop children's co-ordination skills, which will help them as they begin to write.

Mathematics

The maths activities in this book aim to make mathematics an enjoyable and fun experience that children will look forward to. In this area of learning children develop concepts such as big, little, long and short. Through a variety of activities they are encouraged to sort, match and pair animals by colour and other attributes. They learn how to count to ten, handle data and present it in a pictorial form. By singing number songs and rhymes, copying and describing patterns, children begin using and understanding mathematical language while other areas of learning are being developed at the same time.

Science and Technology

This is an exciting and magical area of learning that is full of unexpected events that the children can witness and think about. Good scientific experiences allow children to become active participants in the learning process. They also learn to work as part of a group by talking about and recording what they see – they look at equipment, share ideas and make predictions and observations. In this area of learning, children start to understand a number of different concepts about materials, such as solid and liquid, dry and wet. They develop knowledge of the needs of animals, domestic and wild. In addition, they

discover what farm and working animals provide us with and how we in turn need to care for animals. Children learn through play, using materials of all kinds, or constructional toys, to create their own models, and by selecting the best materials for a job. There are also activities in which they can discover how to use technology, such as stereo cassette recorders.

Time and Place.

This area of learning develops children's language about events and different places. The activities bring some of the world's animals closer to the children's experience. Each activity encourages them to talk about events in their own lives and to help them empathise with animals. Activities that focus on an environment, such as a farm, help to develop children's sense of different places and give them opportunities to compare it with their own environment.

Creative Development

This area of learning enables children to develop their imaginations and to express a response in ways other than by paper and pencil. In the activities, they work with a variety of materials such as egg shells, feathers and other items from nature, as well as found objects like string and glitter. This develops fine motor skills, which will help them as they start finding out how to write. Spatial awareness is extended by using shape, colour and form in 2D and 3D work. Children are also given a variety of opportunities to respond to and discuss stories, songs and rhymes.

Physical Development

This area of learning covers ways in which children can develop gross motor skills by stretching, jumping, rolling, skipping, running, starting, stopping, balancing, throwing and catching and through imaginative movement. It teaches children to work safely with other children and use specialised PE equipment. Physical development also concentrates on developing fine motor skills through sewing, painting, drawing, sticking, cutting, and colouring. Activities that promote this area of learning will also aid the development of emergent writing in language and literacy and will support many of the aims found in personal and social development by encouraging children to work cooperatively alongside their peers.

Assessment

There should be an on-going programme of assessment in the nursery which informs nursery staff and parents where a child stands at the time of assessment, and indicates any particular educational needs. Assessment is a planning tool and should be an integral part of the teaching and learning process. Opportunities for assessment should be identified and included in weekly planning. Assessment should be seen in a positive light informing nursery staff what a child can do rather than what a child cannot do. Without assessment it is impossible to know what learning has taken place. Aims must be clear before the assessment begins. It is useful to have a checklist of expected outcomes with space for comments. The expected outcomes should be kept to a minimum for the observation to be effective. Each activity in this book emphasises more than one area of learning, expressed as a learning outcome. Choose no more than two to assess at a time, to make the assessment manageable. When carrying out an assessment, the way children are questioned is crucial. Ask open-ended questions to find out what the children are thinking or feeling. The questions should do the following: lead the children to review ideas – why did that happen?; promote investigation – which powder will give the cleanest wash?; ask children to justify ideas or actions – why?; encourage self evaluation – how could you make the ball bounce higher?; provide information about children's understanding and misunderstanding – how does it work? At the end of an activity, finished products should be evaluated as soon as possible after they have been produced so that if anything is unclear you can ask the children about what they have done. Classroom management is vital. The amount of time to be spent observing children must be considered. Children not involved in the assessment must be able to play or work independently or with another adult for this time.

Findings should be recorded during or immediately after the observation. Finally, make sure you have a range of assessment strategies and make use of parents and carers' knowledge of their children in the observation and assessment process.

How to use this book

All About Animals is divided into seven self-contained chapters that develop one avenue of the book's central theme. Each chapter has its own coloured bands to help you identify which chapter you are in and its own contents list. The contents list gives you a summary of each activity to help you decide which activities to use. The materials needed for each activity are always found at the top left of the activity and the educational aims are underneath.

Educational symbols

Each activity introduces one or more areas of learning. The symbols show you which areas are covered and the accompanying text gives you the specific aims.

 This symbol shows the activity will develop aspects of language and literacy

 This symbol shows the activity will develop aspects of science and technology

 This symbol shows the activity will develop aspects of creative development

 This symbol shows the activity will develop aspects of mathematics

 This symbol shows the activity will develop aspects of personal and social development

 This symbol shows the activity will develop aspects of physical development

 This symbol shows the activity will develop aspects of time and place

Each activity is numbered for easy reference.

The triangle and circle show you the suggested adult–child ratio for the activity.

3 Frog lifecycle

Materials and preparation
frog lifecycle puzzles · picture books · models of a tadpole and frog

- To explore and recognise features of living things
- To treat living things with care and concern
- To develop a sense of time passing and developmental change by studying what occurs in the lifecycle of a frog
- Extend the activity by talking about the lifecycle of a butterfly

Start this activity by visiting your local pond and studying its pond life.

WHAT TO DO
Lay the materials on the table. Show the children models of a tadpole and a fully-grown frog. Explain to them that the adult frog was once a tadpole. Talk through the whole lifecycle of the frog with the children.

Questions
- What happens to frogspawn?
- Where do tadpoles live?
- Where do frogs live?
- At which time of year do you think frogs lay spawn?

Repeat this activity in the spring so that the children can observe frogspawn developing into tadpoles.

4 Frog stones

Materials and preparation
pictures and models of frogs and their habitats for the children to refer to · pebbles from the beach or garden · green, black and white paint · paint brushes · PVA glue or clear varnish

- To paint on a different material
- To develop an awareness of the concepts of same and different

1 Show pictures and models of frogs. Ask the children why they think frogs have particular features such as long back legs.

Develop children's observational skills by showing them how to make pebble frogs.

2 Talk about frogs' colouring and the patterns on their skin. Show the children pictures of their natural habitats and explain how their skin camouflages them.

3 Paint the pebble green, then add the frog's features and its eyes. Once the paint is dry, brush PVA glue on to the frog to make it smooth and shiny.

TIP · Make paper lily pads for the frogs to sit on. Put these on blue card to represent a pond. If there are no pebbles available make your own by modelling clay into a ball.

Questions
- What colour is a frog?
- Where does a frog live?
- Can you eat frogs?
- What do frogs like to eat?
- What do you think a frog's skin feels like?
- What colour are the spots on frogs?

28

5 The Very Hungry Caterpillar

- To count to 10 with objects. To use mathematical language to describe shape, position and quantity
- To use a growing vocabulary to express thoughts and to listen and respond to stories

This activity is based on 'The Very Hungry Caterpillar' by Eric Carle, published by Puffin.

WHAT TO DO
Read the book to the children and then talk about the changes the caterpillar undergoes. Re-read the section on what the caterpillar eats then ask the children to 'read' each page in turn using the pictures as a visual prompt. Photocopy this section and ask the children to sequence the pages in number order.

Buy an extra copy of the book. Cut out the sequencing pages, laminate or cover them with sticky-backed plastic and stick them on to card.

Questions
- What did the caterpillar eat first/next/last?
- How many apples did the caterpillar eat?
- How many things did the caterpillar eat?
- What did the caterpillar turn into?

6 Spongy caterpillar

Materials and preparation
two circular sponges · two colours of paint · dishes for paint · sugar paper · sponge cut into the shape of a butterfly · black felt-tipped pen

- To respond to a rhyme and begin to associate sounds with patterns in rhymes
- To name and recognise colours and to create simple repeating patterns

Printing a caterpillar shape will develop children's understanding of repeating patterns.

Don't cry caterpillar

Don't cry caterpillar
Caterpillar don't cry
You'll be a butterfly by and by.
Caterpillar please
don't worry 'bout a thing -
'But', said the caterpillar,
'Will I still know myself in wings?'

WHAT TO DO
- Introduce the 'Don't cry caterpillar' rhyme to the children and ask the questions below.
- Encourage the children to create their own spongy caterpillar by printing the caterpillar's body in two repeating colours. Using the butterfly sponge create two butterflies above the caterpillar. Add the finishing touches using a felt-tipped pen to draw feet and antennae.

EXTENSION IDEAS
- Print a caterpillar and butterfly using different print media such as potatoes, leaves and thumb prints.
- Cut out your spongy caterpillar and attach two straws. Make a puppet with which to act out the rhyme.

Questions
- How does a caterpillar move?
- What do caterpillars eat?
- Where have you seen a caterpillar?
- What does a caterpillar turn into.

29

Additional symbols

Many activities have additional hints and tips or safety points. They are identified by the symbols shown below.

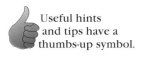 Useful hints and tips have a thumbs-up symbol.

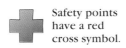 Safety points have a red cross symbol.

Breaking down the information

Each activity either has step-by-step instructions or bullet-pointed instructions under the heading 'What To Do'. Many activities also have suggested questions and extension ideas, also under the appropriate headings.

 TIP One or more helpful suggestions for increasing an activity's learning value have a star symbol.

Planning your theme

The topic of animals is always extremely successful with young children as they are able to relate to animals with ease. All the activities in this book will engage and motivate the children to learn what animals do, where they live and how we can look after them. Remember that some of the children may have experiences of animals before they come to the nursery whereas others may have had no experience of them whatsoever.

As with any other type of learning, it is vital that we allow children to draw on their personal experiences of animals and share them with others. This book is carefully planned so that you begin with the children's own experiences of pets then, as they become more confident, you can encourage them to look at the different animals of the world. You can refer children who have no experience of animals to a wealth of story books and organise volunteers to bring animals to the nursery to meet the children.

When planning an animal theme, it is vital that we cater for the different learning modes that children use: auditory, visual and physical. These include learning through listening to others, learning from pictures and artefacts, and learning from hands-on involvement (vital in the early learning years). The activities on the following pages bring these learning modes into practice.

Preparing for Visits

All visits must be carefully planned so that the day runs smoothly and every effort is made to provide learning opportunities for the children. It is important to decide exactly how the visit fits into the overall development of the theme. This book shows how a visit to a farm can be a powerful stimulus for the children. Before taking children to a farm, however, it is important that members of staff make an initial visit together. This will enable staff to consider safety and organisational aspects such as whether the animals are in enclosures and if there is a place where children can find shelter if it rains and facilities for washing hands after touching animals and before eating. The book also gives teachers and supervisors the information they need to carry out with confidence activities that they might otherwise decide not to undertake.

Before making a visit anywhere, always consult the nursery's policy on taking children beyond the nursery building. A letter home to parents or carers giving details of the visit is also essential. Include information on appropriate clothes and footwear to be worn by the children and guidance on food and drink – for example no glass bottles. Put a plea out for adult help so that the children can be divided into very small groups.

On the day of the visit give all the adults who are participating a list of the children's names and their contact numbers. Also give each adult a separate list of the children's names he or she is supervising that day and an itinerary. Write down some useful questions that they could ask the children to promote meaningful discussion. It is often useful not to be supervising a group of children yourself so that you can interact with all the children and be able to take photographs of them or film them using a video camera. Each child should wear a badge showing your nursery's name and telephone number. Take a first aid pack and any inhalers or medicines that the children may require with you, too.

Before going on the visit talk to the children about what they will do on the day and what you hope they will see and find out about. Make sure the children have had an opportunity to go to the toilet before you leave. Talk to them about safety rules and your expectations of their behaviour.

Nursery Visitors

It is important not to overlook the possibility of asking visitors to the nursery to show the children types of animal that they may not otherwise meet – guide dogs, police dogs or simply pet animals they may not have at home. Put up a notice asking any parents who work with animals, such farmers, vets, pet shop assistants and so on, if they are prepared to come into the nursery to talk to the children about their work. You can also contact animal organisations, who will send useful free information and posters on request. In addition, many offer free educational visits. Visitors to the nursery must be escorted by nursery staff at all times.

Asking questions

Discussion is vital if you are to develop the children's thinking. This book is full of questions that will help your children think about the various issues concerning animals. It is important that you help the children to listen attentively to others when they are answering a question and to take turns when speaking.

Think carefully about the type of questions you ask. Questions can be broadly divided into two main types: 'open' and 'closed'. Most of the questions suggested with the activities in this book are of the 'open' type. Open questions differ from closed questions by inviting a range of acceptable, often longer, responses. For example, an open question may often begin with words such as 'why do you think that...', so that the child is encouraged to consider all aspects of the subject under discussion and to express a personal point of view. By contrast, a closed question only requires a short response. A typical closed question is, 'Do you like dogs?' A simple 'yes' or 'no' answer is all that is required and the child is not encouraged to think about the reasons for his or her response.

Closed questions have many disadvantages over the open variety. The majority of closed questions have only one correct or anticipated answer. They can engender the idea in children that learning is about finding 'the one correct answer'. They can also, through repeated use, lead the children to guess the answer or word that they think the teacher is expecting.

In contrast open questions require more planning. Children also need longer to formulate their responses.

Open questions require more complex management in large group situations as they invite more diverse and longer responses than closed questions.

Open questions can offer children more opportunities for creative thinking. They may also provide the teacher with insights into individual children's understanding, and be used to guide children to take another step forwards in their learning. Open questions can often challenge children's thinking and motivate them to become positively involved in activities. They can also be effective in encouraging children to develop certain skills. During storytime, for example, the teacher might ask a child to predict by asking what will happen next.

Asking their own questions

Introducing a theme and asking questions motivates children to take a greater interest in the world around them. Not only will the right questioning encourage them to consider their responses carefully but they will develop the ability to ask questions of their own. These may be directed at their teacher when thinking about the subject under discussion. In addition, they will learn to ask one another questions – developing enquiring minds and a sense of living within a diverse society. They will learn, through questioning, to interact with other children and develop good social skills. This will serve to increase their knowledge and understanding, and they will become more eloquent and expressive in their dealings with others. Their learning ability will also be enhanced as they discover how interesting the world around them is. All the questions suggested in this book will promote this enthusiasm for knowledge.

Topic web

Each activity in this book is underpinned by one or more areas of learning. This topic web lists all the activities that develop each area of learning under the appropriate heading. Use this web when planning your curriculum to ensure the activities you use develop all areas of learning according to the particular early years guidelines you are following. This will help you create an educationally exciting and balanced theme that your children will love!

CREATIVE DEVELOPMENT

LANGUAGE AND LITERACY

TIME AND PLACE

SCIENCE AND TECHNOLOGY

MATHEMATICS

PERSONAL AND SOCIAL DEVELOPMENT

PHYSICAL DEVELOPMENT

PETS

The activities in this chapter are based on the types of animals that children have most experience of – pets. Children are encouraged to develop an understanding of the differing needs of a variety of pets and how to look after and care for them. The projects provide many opportunities to create strong links between the children's homes and the nursery, and with the local neighbourhood, too. As with all activities involving animals, always ensure that you are aware of any children who are afraid of animals and tailor the activities you ask them to participate in accordingly. Finally, always aim to develop the children's sensitivity to the welfare of animals they study or keep as pets.

Activities in this chapter

1
Pet portraits
Children will love drawing their pet after closely observing a photograph

2
Pets in a flap
An activity that introduces children to the concept of lift-the-flap books – how they work and how to make them

3
Singing time
An interactive singing activity that teaches children the sounds that different animals make

4
Approaching pets
Children are taught how to approach animals and how their behaviour may scare animals

5
Animal hospital
A fun role play activity that will involve all the nursery children whether they have a pet at home or not

6
Animal survey
This activity introduces simple mathematical concepts in the form of a survey

7
Keeping a nursery pet
Children develop an understanding of how any pet needs daily care and attention, and use their creativity to make a ballot box so that the group can choose the pet's name together

8
Looking after pets
In this activity, a toy pet is used to introduce the principles involved in looking after pets

9
Where's our cat?
Children find out how to use writing for different purposes, and how to make a poster to help to find a lost cat

1 Pet portraits

Materials and preparation

photographs of pets · pencils
crayons · white A4 paper
strips of card · glue

 To talk about photographs

 To enjoy exploring the properties of pencils and crayons

 To understand descriptive language and join in discussion

Questions

What does your pet look like?
What colour are your pet's eyes?
What do you think is special about your pet?
What is your pet called?

A sk the children and their parents to bring in photographs of their pets for this activity.

Bring in extra photographs for children who forget to bring in any of their own or who do not have access to photographs.

WHAT TO DO

- Lay out all the animal photographs with the children sitting in a circle on the floor around them.
- Pick up one of the photographs and describe the pet.
- Now ask the children to do the same.
- Ask the children to draw a picture of any one of the pets they choose.

EXTENSION IDEAS

- Show the children how to make a collage frame for their portraits, using strips of card to stick around the edges. The frame can be decorated using crayons.

2 Pets in a flap

Materials and preparation

'Spot' books by Eric Hill, published by Penguin
white A4 paper · pencils
crayons · scissors
clear sticky tape

 To enjoy looking at books
To understand that (in English) print runs from left to right

 To talk freely with other adults and children

B ase this activity on one of the Spot lift-the-flap books, showing how a flap book is made.

1 Show the children how the flap book works. Explain that the flap must cover the animal.

2 Show the children how to make a lift-the-flap page then let them make their own.

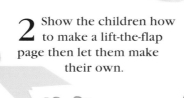

WHAT TO DO

- Read a lift-the-flap book to the children. Talk about how they could make a group flap book. Decide on an animal story character and where you are going to hide it. Let the children make one page each for the book. Follow steps one to three.

3 Staple together the pages to make a group book and leave it out, so the children can refer to it.

3 Singing time

Materials and preparation

- percussion instruments to accompany the song

 To listen and to respond to rhyme

 To participate in group activities led by an adult

 To use their imagination when making music

Questions

- Can you think of any other animals that could be included in the song?
- What do you like most about the song?
- Can you clap the rhythm of the song?

Extend the activity by asking the children to choose an animal to draw. Tell them to annotate the picture with the name of the animal and their own name.

Choose a tune the children are familiar with to accompany this song.

I've got a dog

I've got a dog
a very special dog
and he goes everywhere with me,
With a woof here,
a woof there
and a woof, woof everywhere.

▸ WHAT TO DO

- Firstly, teach the childre the tune to the song. Then follow steps one to three for the words.
- Ask the children to mak up their own actions.
- Tell them to join in by playing a percussion instrument.

1 I've got a dog, a very special dog and he goe everywhere with me. With woof here ...

2 I've got a cat, a very special cat and she goe everywhere with me. With meow ...

3 I've got a bird, a very special bird and it goes everywhere with me. With chirp here ...

4 Approaching pets

 To be confident in a new situation

 To be able to talk freely with familiar adults

Let parents know when you are planning to run this activity and ensure you are aware of any children who are scared of animals.

Ensure children understand they should not approach unknown animals on their own.

Contact local animal welfare organisations for information. Find out whether it is possible for someone to come in and talk to the children.

Use this activity to remind children that pets are not toys and that they should be treated as living animals with feelings.

▸ WHAT TO DO

- Ask a parent who owns a docile dog to bring it into the nursery.
- Introduce the children the dog and explain wh they should approach animals with care. Explain that animals ca get scared, too and that if the children approach an animal too quickly they may frighten it.
- Allow the children to approach the dog in small groups and stroke it. Explain that the dog shows that it is feeling pleased and happy by wagging its tail and that dogs do not like their tails being pulled.

5 Animal hospital

U se this activity to encourage children to foster a caring attitude to animals.

Materials and preparation

variety of soft animal toys · bandages · plasters · toy vet's equipment such as stethescopes · a table · white overalls · pencil · note pad (for prescriptions) · telephone (to take appointments)

To listen when others are speaking

To develop a caring attitude. To enjoy playing alongside other children

▶ WHAT TO DO

- Turn the role play corner into a veterinary surgery. Set up a waiting room with a few chairs. Place the soft toys on the chairs, waiting for attention. Add a treatment table with bandages and plasters.
- Let the children who are playing the roles of staff put on white coats.
- Interact with the children by sitting in the waiting room with your own soft toy. Tell the them what is wrong with the toy – perhaps he has a sore tail or paw.

EXTENSION IDEAS

Contact the animal welfare organisations listed in the resources section on page 59 and ask for suitable posters to decorate the surgery.
Show the children how to tie bandages, so that they can try bandaging their toy animals.

Questions

- Can you help my pet?
- How can I make my pet better?
- How much will the treatment cost?
- Will I have to bring him back to the surgery?

👍 Show the children how to make appointments to ensure owners and pets are seen in turn and are not kept waiting for too long.

TIP Ask someone from your local veterinary surgery to come into the nursery to talk to the children about what his or her work involves.

👍 Ensure the children take it in turns to be vet and the pet's owner.

Animal survey

Materials and preparation

· pictures of pet animals from books or magazines for reference · sugar paper · crayons · paints · paintbrushes

To count with objects to 10. To use mathematical language such as more and less

To pose a question and find the answer

Questions

· How many children already have a pet/would like to own a pet?
· How many have/would like to own dogs?
· How many have/would like to own cats?
· Which is the most popular pet to own?

This activity introduces the children to organising items into categories as they decide which animal they would most like to own.

▶ WHAT TO DO

· Ask the children to draw a picture of the type of pet that they would most like to own. Give them pictures they can refer to
· Suggest some suitable pets to them – a dog, cat, rabbit, guinea pig, gerbil or goldfish. Which would be their favourite?
· Now sort the pictures into categories for each type of pet that the children have drawn.
· Everyone counts the pictures in each category to find out which type of pet is the most popular.
· Ask each child to say why he or she chose the pet they did. Was it because they already have, say, a dog or cat at home? Perhaps they have read about an animal in a story

---

Keeping a nursery pet

Materials and preparation

· Water bowl or tank · goldfish · fish food · small ballot box · pieces of paper · pencils

To make observations

To express an idea and discuss choice of names

To count with objects

Questions

· Ask the children questions so that they take an interest in the fish
· What does the fish look like?
· Why do you think we should name the fish?

A goldfish is an ideal pet for introducing the children to looking after another living being. As a follow-on activity, they can all help to choose a name for it.

Spot
Jaws
Goldy

▶ WHAT TO DO

· Tell the children that, like them, the goldfish needs to eat regularly. Organise for them to take turns to feed it. This can be a group activity in which the other children gather round, and you describe how the fish swims and breathes under water.
· Make a rota for each child to take care of the fish at weekends. Check that parents will agree to this
· Ask the children to think up a name for the fish. Scribe the names. Let the children post them in the ballot box to find the most popular name

You could carry out this activity using another suitable nursery pet.

8   Looking after pets

Materials and preparation

* toy dog · grooming tools · lead collar · bowl with food · drinking bowl · dog treats

To share their experiences of looking after a pet and join in group discussion

To work together to look after a pet and be aware of its needs

Place a toy dog in the home corner and let the children work together to care for it.

EXTENSION IDEAS

Let the children talk about how they care for their pet at home, and the types of pet they care for. What are the different requirements of these animals? Do cats need walking? Do dogs like playing with balls?

Stress the importance of working together and that looking after a pet is easier if tasks are shared.

Questions

* What does it need?
* How are we going to care for it? Can we look after it?
* Does it have special needs?
* Are its needs different to other pets?

WHAT TO DO

* Talk about pet dogs and how and why we need to care for them.
* List the tasks for looking after a dog, such as feeding, grooming, exercising, and preparing for bed.
* Let the children decide who is going to be responsible for each task.

---

9   Where's our cat?

Materials and preparation

* sugar paper · large piece of thin card · paints · paint brushes · crayons · glue · pet toy

To use writing to convey messages

To observe the features of a pet and recreate its image in paint

To participate in group activities led by an adult

This activity looks at how to think of ways of finding a lost animal.

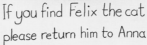

WHAT TO DO

* Before the children arrive hide the toy pet.
* Talk to the children about how they could tell people their pet is lost.
* Suggest making a lost pet poster and explain what it would need to say.
* Make the poster as a group so that every child can contribut ideas.
* Ask the children to suggest where the best place would be to put the poster.
* The next day, put the pet in a prominent place, so the children can find it.

FARM ANIMALS

The activities in this chapter will help children learn about animal families. For example, there are step-by-step instructions on how children can have an action-packed day on the farm and learn about lambing as well as seeing hens with their chicks. The day out and the accompanying projects will develop children's understanding of how special farm animals are and what they provide The lessons the children learnt at the farm can then be reinforced with a variety of activities, including thought-provoking story reading, imitating the sounds made by different animals, and informative craft projects.

Activities in this chapter

1
Farmyard families
Use this activity to tell the children what types of animals live on farms and what different baby animals are called – for example, pigs and piglets, goats and kids, and so on

2
Animal sounds
Children will enjoy participating in this activity, and can be expressive while learning more about animals

3
Which animals are at the farm
Find out how to make a farm visit a richly rewarding experience for children

4
What do we get from animals?
Children can learn about food from farm animals by participating in this activity

5
The Little Red Hen
From this story, children can learn about helping others and working together

6
Hens lay eggs
Once children have enjoyed making this project, they will always remember that hens lay eggs

7
Where do farm animals live?
Reading the children this story will encourage them to think about why farm animals are sometimes outdoors and sometimes indoors

8
Wild or domestic?
In this activity children will develop organisational ability and think about different animals

9
Where do we get milk come from?
By helping to make this cow, children will learn and remember where milk comes from

10
Farmyard sing along
This musical activity will make children think about the sounds made by different farm animals

1 Farmyard families

Materials and preparation

• farm yard toy animals with adults and babies • farm yard books with pictures of adult and baby animals appropriately labelled • paper • pencils • crayons

To use appropriate vocabulary

To record their observations

To be aware that animals have families

To sort objects according to set criteria

TIP • Introduce appropriate language such as, mother, father, bull, cow and calf.

This activity helps the children to realise that, like them, animals have families who look after them.

Make sure you look at your resources before you start and ensure that there is a matching baby to each adult animal.

▶ WHAT TO DO

• Put out all the materials on a table.
• Ask the children to sort the animals into families.
• Encourage them to name the animals and talk to you about them.
• Ask them to choose one family, then draw it on a piece of paper. Supply appropriate reference material, such as books and models. Encourage them to pay careful attention to detail.

---

2 Animal sounds

Materials and preparation

• cassette tape recorder • blank cassette tape • cassette tape with animal sounds • homemade book with pictures of farmyard animals

To join in group activities led by an adult

To listen and respond with sounds, and to explore the onomatapoeic qualities of language

Use a tape that only has 5 minutes running time on it so that you don't spend a long time rewinding it.

Children love to imitate animal sounds and this activity will teach them those of different animals.

▶ WHAT TO DO

• Make an animal sounds book by sticking in pictures of the animal included on the cassette tape. Annotate each picture with a written approximation to the sound the animal makes.
• Show the children each picture in turn and talk about the sounds each animal makes.
• Play the pre-recorded animal sounds tape and let the children imitate the sounds.
• Record all the different animal sounds they make.
• Rewind the tape and let them listen to themselves.
• Leave out the materials so that the children can return to them during free play times.

3 Which animals are at the farm?

Materials and preparation

- A local farm that caters for children's needs and that provides hands-on experience

 To learn about animals and where they live

 To listen attentively and talk about the experience

 To develop a caring attitude towards animals

 To observe specific features

The best way for children to learn about what happens on farms is to organize a hands-on visit with fun activities to do on the day.

👍 A preliminary visit by adults who are going on the trip is vital.

👍 If a farm visit is awkward for your locality, find out about city farms or mobile farms in your area.

TIPS Take photographs of the children with the animals during their trip. These will come in handy when making a big book back at the nursery.

- Talk to the children about their surroundings and provide them with appropriate vocabulary.
- After the trip, have a discussion with the children about what the animals were actually doing. Were they playing, sleeping and so on?

👍 You could arrange a zoo trip afterwards to compare the differences between the animals. If possible, visit a small, child-friendly zoo.

▶ **WHAT TO DO**

- Start by finding out when the farm is able to accommodate a large group of children.
- Book your day and inform the children's parents well in advance.
- Ensure you have a high adult:child ratio for the outing and that parents provide their children with clothes for all kinds of weather.
- Pack a first-aid kit and if possible take a qualified first aider.
- Take a change of clothes in case a child has an accident.
- Prepare an itinerary and give a copy to each adult so they know the exact plans for the day.

✚ Talk to the children before the visit about handling and touching animals safely.

Questions

- Which animals do you think will be at the farm?
- What do you want to see at the farm?
- Where is the farm?
- Have you been to a farm before and what did you see then?
- What did you see on the way to the farm?

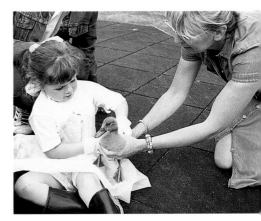

TIPS • Make sure there is a covered area under which you can shelter in case it rains. Telephone the farm in advance to find out when feeding times are and check that the children can watch these events. If possible, arrange the visit during the spring so that the children can gain understanding of lambing and the birth of chicks.

A farm tour will develop children's basic knowledge of life on a farm.

Make sure the children understand that farm animals are not pets and should be treated differently.

Ensure that the children wash their hands before eating. Stress to them during the day how important it is that they do not put their fingers in their mouths after touching the animals.

▶ WHAT TO DO

• Split your party into small groups and send them to different parts of the farm to observe the animals. This will enable the children to see and touch the animals, while ensuring that the animals are not intimidated or scared by a crowd.
• Encourage the children to draw the animals they observe using their paper and clipboards.
• Encourage the children to collect their farm treasures in the plastic cups you have provided.
• Try to organize a talk by one of the farm workers and let the children ask questions.

EXTENSION IDEAS

Make thank you cards with the children after the visit that they can send to the farm workers.
• Ask the children to bring in their cup of treasures and talk about each item.
• Make a nursery book using the photographs taken during the visit.

Questions

• How many different kinds of animals are at the farm?
• Which is your favourite animal and why?
• Who looks after the animals?
• Are there any baby animals at the farm?
• Are any of the animals working?
• What do the animals eat?
• What sort of noises can you hear?

What do we get from animals?

Materials and preparation

• honeycomb • goat's/cow's/sheep's milk/cheese /yoghurt • goose/duck/hen/quail eggs • raw and knitting wool • feathers from a variety of birds feather products such as dusters • plates and bowls to put the items in • spoons to taste the items • card and pen for labels

 To sort by set criteria, and understand basic concepts such as same/different and big/little

 To show interest and feel confident tasting new kinds of food

 To understand the need for washing hands before and after handling food

 To talk about and react to different tastes, smells and textures

This is a good way to explain to children why we have farm animals.

▶ WHAT TO DO

• Before encouraging the children to taste farm produce, check with their parents so that you are aware of any religious or cultural prohibitions.
• Divide the items into two groups: those that we eat and those that we don't. Label and place them on separate tables.
• Working in small groups, start with the farm animal products we eat. Talk about each item.
• Start by tasting the milk, then ask the children to predict what the yoghurt and cheese will taste like. Remind them these items are made from milk.
• Taste the honeycomb next. Talk about how it is made by bees.

▶ WHAT TO DO

• Now introduce the items from farm animals that we do not eat but which have other important uses.
• Talk about each item in turn, concentrating on what the natural product is turned into. Tell them duck feathers are used for dusters and to fill pillows. Show them untreated wool shorn from sheep and a ball of knitting wool.

Place the eggs next to each other so that the children can compare the relative sizes.

Stress that the children must not try to taste any of the inedible items. You may prefer to boil the eggs before the activity.

TIP • Have life-size pictures of a duck, hen, goose and quail to hand. Compare the relative bird sizes with their eggs.
• Use items collected during the farm visit to help reinforce the children's learning.

EXTENSION IDEAS

• Comb the raw fleece into strands, then twist the strands into threads. In this way the children can see and understand how wool is made.

The Little Red Hen

To enjoy listening to a story and to participate in a question and answer session

To be helpful to others.

Introduce the concept of everyone working together by reading 'The Little Red Hen.'

EXTENSION IDEAS

Make some bread with the children.
Bring in some corn cobs and explain how the corn is dried and ground to make flour.

▶ WHAT TO DO

- Read 'The Little Red Hen' by Alan Garner, Dorling Kindersley, and ask the questions below.

Questions

- Have you ever made bread?
- What do you need to make bread?
- Why should they have helped the little red hen?
- How do you think the little red hen felt?
- Do you help people do things?
- Which is your favourite character in the book?

Hens lay eggs

Materials and preparation
- pencil • coloured card for the hen
- cup and plate to draw around
- scissors • feathers • PVA glue
- felt-tipped pens • stapler
- hard-boiled eggs

To discover how different materials can be used in a craft activity

To reinforce the idea that hens lay eggs

Continue your theme of animal products from the farm visit with this craft project.

Colour the beak and comb with felt-tipped pen.

1 Draw around the cup for the head and the bowl for the body. Add the beak, comb, and tail, then cut out.

2 Add the feathers on to the body and tail. Cut out another body-sized circle.

Questions

How do you eat your eggs – boiled, poached or fried?
What else can we make with eggs?
Which other animals lay eggs?
What sounds do hens make?
What do eggs look like?

3 Staple the top and sides of the second circle to the body of the hen. Leave an opening at the base to sit the hen on the hard-boiled eggs.

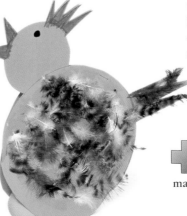

▶ 3WHAT TO DO

- Introduce the activity by asking the children where eggs come from. They will hopefully remember from their farm visit. Remind them that hens are female and that cockerels do not lay eggs. Did they see cockerels on their farm visit? Where do hens like to lay their eggs? Ask them to name any other birds that live on farms and lay eggs. Do they remember seeing ducks on the farm?
- Lay out all the materials on a table and follow steps one to three with the children to make hens to sit on hard-boiled eggs. The children will be sure to remember where eggs come from!

✚ Hard boil the eggs to reduce the risk of salmonella and to make them more robust.

7   Where do farm animals live?

Materials and preparation

* farm animal set that has a range of animals kept in different places such as barns, pens, stys and so on

EXTENSION IDEA

Talk about why animals come inside in the winter and how the farm buildings are insulated with straw. Make pens for the farm animals to sleep in.

Introduce this activity by reading 'Farmyard Animals' by Paul Hess, Zero to Ten.

 To share ideas with others and to clarify their thinking

 To sort objects according to specified criteria

To play purposefully alongside other children

▶ WHAT TO DO

* Read the book and then study the farm picture at the back. Point out where all the animals are. Talk about where the animals go during the day and where they go at night.
* Show the children the toy animals and ask them to sort the animals using their own criteria. For example, they could decide to place all the animals inside the farm buildings or to put them in various fields to graze. Ask the children to explain why they are putting each type of animal where.

8   Wild or domestic?

Materials and preparation

* wild and domestic toy animals
* one label that says wild and one that says domestic

To sort objects according to set criteria

To concentrate and work alongside other children

To listen when another child is speaking, share points of view and exchange ideas

Questions

* Why are farm animals domestic?
* What do we get from farm animals?
* Do we get anything from wild animals?
* Where do we find wild animals?
* Which farm animals have you seen?

This mathematical activity encourages children to think about the differences between animals.

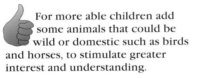 For more able children add some animals that could be wild or domestic such as birds and horses, to stimulate greater interest and understanding.

▶ WHAT TO DO

* Lay all the toy animals on the table and talk about each animal in turn. Ask the children to name the animals and if they know where they come from.
* Talk about the differences between wild and domestic animals, and explain both these terms carefully.
* Ask the children to work in pairs to sort the animals into two groups – wild and domestic.

Where do we get milk from?

Materials and preparation

• organise a farm visit in which children can see cows being milked and hopefully also see calves drinking their mothers's milk or being bottle fed

 To participate in group activities led by an adult

 To participate in question-and-answer sessions led by an adult

You can use this as a follow-on activity to the farm visit suggested on page 20.

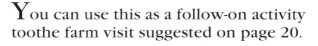

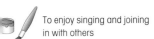 The Mobile Little Folks Farm in Hertfordshire will bring animals to the nursery and let the children bottle feed a calf. Contact your Local Education Authority for details.

WHAT TO DO

• If possible, visit a farm where the children can see a cow being milked. At calving time, it should also be possible to see calves drinking their mothers' milk or being bottle fed.

• Talk to the children about how cows produce milk for their calves and how we also drink this milk.

• Explain that, in the past, milking was carried out by people but that it is now mainly done with milking machines. Tell them that the cows' udders are squeezed and that milk squirts out through teets into containers placed beneath the cows. Reassure the children that this process is completely comfortable for cows, who are glad not to have full udders!

Farmyard sing along

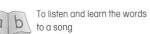 To listen and learn the words to a song

To enjoy singing and joining in with others

Songs and rhymes are ideal starting points for talking about different farmyard animals.

Old MacDonald had a farm

WHAT TO DO

• Teach the children the words to the song.

• Ask the children which is their favourite farmyard animal.

• Ask the children which they think is the noisiest farmyard animal.

• Ask the children which they think is the quietest.

• Ask the children to act out the rhyme.

• Recreate the song with your farm set with the children picking up the appropriate animal when they sing.

MINI BEASTS

The activities in this chapter help to develop children's knowledge of science and nature. They are given the opportunity to discover different forms of wildlife, including insects and amphibians. First-hand experiences of mini beasts encourage children to have caring attitudes towards animals that are smaller than themselves. The children will love making their very own mini beasts and using them to act out informative stories and rhymes. They will also gain an understanding of the different lifecycles of certain creatures, such as frogs and caterpillars, which will enable them to form an interest in the natural world.

Activities in this chapter

1
Fly ladybird fly
Children love ladybirds and will enjoy learning this simple rhyme

2
Flying ladybirds
This follow-on activity to Fly ladybird fly will encourage the children to think about how insects use their wings to fly

3
Frog lifecycle
By learning how frogs develop from tadpoles, children will gain an awareness of stages in some unusual lifecycles

4
Frog stones
Children will enjoy making their own frogs and toads, and the activity will develop their perceptive skills

5
The Very Hungry Caterpillar
Reading this story will make the children aware of how a caterpillar becomes a butterfly

6
Spongy caterpillar
Encourage children to think more about caterpillars and develop their creative skills with this printing project

7
Snail tank
This activity is ideal for developing children's interest in nature and teaching them to take care of other living creatures

8
Snail spirals
By having fun making a snail picture with a spiralled string shell, children will learn how to form patterns

9
Busy spiders
Reading a story about a busy spider helps the children to think about why spiders spin webs

10
Springy spiders' webs
This follow-on activity to Busy Spiders makes the children think about what a spider's web looks like

1 Fly ladybird fly

Children love to recite favourite rhymes, and this type of activity introduces them to verse and rhyming words.

Materials and preparation

selection of pictures to look at including ladybirds and other mini beasts.

To listen and respond to a rhyme

Ladybird, Ladybird

Ladybird, Ladybird, fly away home,

Your house is on fire and
your children all gone;

All but one, and her name is Ann,

And she crept under the frying pan.

▶ WHAT TO DO

- Teach the children the words of the rhyme
- Ask them to recite the rhyme slowly then quickly and to add hand actions.
- Talk to the children about how a ladybird flies. What does it use? Explain to them how a ladybird has wings under its bright red or yellow spotted wing cases.
- Talk about other minibeasts that fly.

---

2 Flying ladybirds

Make these ladybirds as a follow-on activity to Fly ladybird fly (1) page 27.

Materials and preparation

one copy of ladybird templates on page 60 for each child · pencil · black card · scissors · PVA glue · red card · black paint · split pins · white crayon

To explore different materials

To be able to handle scissors and control a paint brush

To count and match shapes

EXTENSION IDEAS

Make the ladybirds from felt and cut out spots for the wing cases from black felt. Attach pieces of Velcro to the wing cases and to the back of the spots. Ask the children to fix the spots in place. How many are there?

➕ Ensure that adults push the split pins through the card to prevent any stabbing of fingers.

1 Trace around the body and leg templates on to black card. Cut out all the pieces. Glue the legs on to the body, pressing firmly.

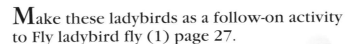

You will need three pairs of legs for each child

2 Trace around the wing case template on to red card. Cut out two wings. Paint black spots on the wings.

3 Using split pins, fasten the wings to the body at the edge of either side so that the wings can swing open. Add the eyes and mouth with white crayon.

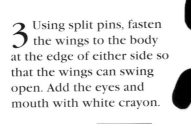

▶ WHAT TO DO

- Follow steps one to three to make the ladybirds. Cut out discs from black card to make spots for the wing cases. Attach small pieces of Blu-Tak to the backs of the discs. Encourage the children to match the discs with the painted spots. Tell them to count how many spots there are. Ask if they have noticed how the spots form a pattern. Is the pattern symmetrical? Explain what this means.

3   Frog lifecycle

Materials and preparation
- frog lifecycle puzzles · picture books
- models of a tadpole and frog

To explore and recognise features of living things

To treat living things with care and concern

To develop a sense of time passing and developmental change by studying what occurs in the lifecyle of a frog

Extend the activity by talking about the lifecycle of a butterfly.

Start this activity by visiting your local pond and studying its pond life.

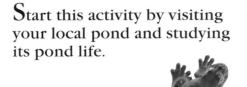

Repeat this activity in the spring so that the children can observe frogspawn developing into tadpoles.

▶ **WHAT TO DO**

- Lay the materials on the table. Show the children models of a tadpole and a fully-grown frog. Explain to them that the adult frog was once a tadpole.
- Talk through the whole lifecycle of the frog with the children.

Questions
- What happens to frogspawn?
- Where do tadpoles live?
- Where do frogs live?
- At which time of year do you think frogs lay spawn?

---

4   Frog stones

Materials and preparation
- pictures and models of frogs and their habitats for the children to refer to
- pebbles from the beach or garden
- green, black and white paint · paint brushes · PVA glue or clear varnish

To paint on a different material

To develop an awareness of the concepts of same and different

1 Show pictures and models of frogs. Ask the children why they think frogs have particular features such as long back legs.

Develop children's observational skills by showing them how to make pebble frogs.

2 Talk about frogs' colouring and the patterns on their skin. Show the children pictures of their natural habitats and explain how their skin camouflages them.

3 Paint the pebble green, then add the frog's features and its eyes. Once the paint is dry, brush PVA glue on to the frog to make it smooth and shiny.

TIP · Make paper lily pads for the frogs to sit on. Put these on blue card to represent a pond.
- If there are no pebbles available make your own by modelling clay into a ball.

Questions
- What colour is a frog?
- Where does a frog live?
- Can you eat frogs?
- What do frogs like to eat?
- What do you think a frog's skin feels like?
- What colour are the spots on frogs?

5   The Very Hungry Caterpillar

 To count to 10 with objects. To use mathematical language to describe shape, position and quantity

 To use a growing vocabulary to express thoughts and to listen and respond to stories

This activity is based on 'The Very Hungry Caterpillar' by Eric Carle, published by Puffin.

Questions

- What did the caterpillar eat first/next/last?
- How many apples did the caterpillar eat?
- How many things did the caterpillar eat?
- What did the caterpillar turn into?

▶ WHAT TO DO

- Read the book to the children and then talk about the changes the caterpillar undergoes.
- Re-read the section on what the caterpillar eats then ask the children to 'read' each page in turn using the pictures as a visual prompt.
- Photocopy this section and ask the children to sequence the pages in number order.

Buy an extra copy of the book. Cut out the sequencing pages, laminate or cover them with sticky-backed plastic and stick them on to card.

6   Spongy caterpillar

Materials and preparation

· two circular sponges · two colours of paint · dishes for paint · sugar paper · sponge cut into the shape of a butterfly · black felt-tipped pen

 To respond to a rhyme and begin to associate sounds with patterns in rhymes

To name and recognise colours and to create simple repeating patterns

Printing a caterpillar shape will develop children's understanding of repeating patterns.

Don't cry caterpillar

Don't cry caterpillar
Caterpillar don't cry
You'll be a butterfly by and by.
Caterpillar please
don't worry 'bout a thing -
'But', said the caterpillar,
'Will I still know myself in wings?'

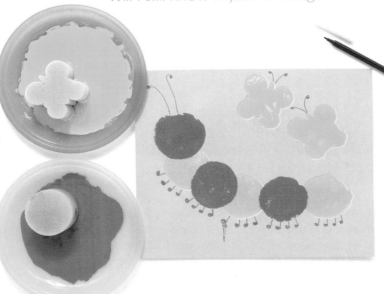

▶ WHAT TO DO

- Introduce the 'Don't cry caterpillar' rhyme to the children and ask the questions below.
- Encourage the children to create their own spongy caterpillar by printing the caterpillar's body in two repeating colours.
- Using the butterfly sponge create two butterflies above the caterpillar. Add the finishing touches using a felt-tipped pen to draw feet and antennae.

EXTENSION IDEAS

- Print a caterpillar and butterfly using different print media such as potatoes, leaves and thumb prints.
- Cut out your spongy caterpillar and attach two straws. Make a puppet with which to act out the rhyme.

Questions

- How does a caterpillar move?
- What do caterpillars eat?
- Where have you seen a caterpillar?
- What does a caterpillar turn into.

7 Snail tank

• old fish tank • leaves and twigs to go in the tank to create a natural environment • netting • food for snails such as lettuce leaves • snails from your garden or park • plastic container • netting • plant spray

 To participate in a question-and-answer session.

To observe and record the behaviour of snails

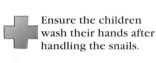 Ensure the children wash their hands after handling the snails.

In this activity, children can observe snails' slithering movements. They are only active when damp, so spray them with water regularly.

Keep a tight elasticised piece of netting over the tank so that the snails can breathe and also so that they do not escape.

▶ WHAT TO DO

• Place the snail tank in a quiet corner of your room. Keep leaves for the snails next to the tank.
• Collect three snails in a plastic container from the garden. Lower the snails gently into the tank. Give them time to adjust to their new environment.
• Introduce the children to the snail tank and give small groups time to observe and record the snails' behaviour.
• Ask them to talk about what they see. Keep the snails for about one week before releasing them back into the wild.

---

8 Snail spirals

Materials and preparation

• pictures of snails for reference • spiral shapes • sugar paper • lengths of string • glue • scissors • paint • paint brushes • felt tipped pen • glitter • snail template on page 60

 To handle appropriate tools with increasing control

 To work with a different material

A project in which children develop their manipulative skills and find out about patterns that occur in the natural world.

Questions

• What pattern is on the snail's shell?
• Can you see any spiral patterns in the nursery?
• What other materials could you use to make the snail's shell?
• Have you noticed the shiny trail a snail leaves behind?

Draw the snail outline and spiral large so that it is easier for the children to stick the string on it.

EXTENSION IDEAS

Encourage the children to collect shells when they go on seaside trips, and to examine the different spiral patterns.
• Ask them to think about the other patterns that occur in nature, such as the rings on a sawn tree trunk and the veins on leaves. Can they think of other patterns?

1 Photocopy and enlarge the snail template. Trace it onto sugar paper – one for each child. Let the children spread glue along the spiral outline.

2 Starting at the centre, trail the string around the spiral pushing it down on the glue. Once the spiral is dry, paint the snail. Add a glitter trail.

Busy spiders

To respond to what they touch and feel, and to use their imagination. To be able to listen and observe

To listen and respond to a story and understand that words and pictures carry meaning

Questions

- What do you think a spider's web feels like?
- Why do you think the web is sticky?
- Where do spiders like to spin their webs?

This activity is based on 'The very busy spider' by Eric Carle, Penguin books.

WHAT TO DO

- Read the story to the children encouraging them to feel the spider's web on the pages.
- Ask if they have ever seen a spider's web and if so where was it.
- Talk about how the spider spins its web and the triangle shapes it makes as it is spinning its web.
- Take the children outside to look for spiders' webs.

---

10 Springy spider's web

Materials and preparation

- large plate · plastic cup · light coloured crayon or chalk · scissors · pipe clearners · hole puncher · elastaic thread

To handle tools appropriately and with increasing control

To use mathematical language when describing a piece of work

TIP · Ensure the children draw the web on both sides of the large circle so that the web is seen from all angles when hanging up.
· Spray the chalk with hair spray to stop it smudging.

EXTENSION IDEAS

- Make a huge spider's web on the wall. Decorate it with glitter. Ask the children to make their own spiders and stick them on to the web.

This activity can be used as a follow-up to Busy spiders (9) page 31.

1 For the spider's web, draw around a bowl on to black card. For the spider's body, draw around a yoghurt pot. Then cut out the large and small circles.

2 Ask the children to draw a spiral pattern on the large circle. Draw diagonal lines from the centre to the edge. Punch holes at the top and bottom of the web.

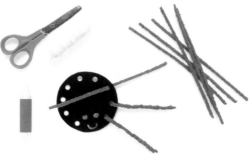

3 Punch nine holes around the small circle, eight for the legs and one for the elastic. Thread the pipe cleaners half-way through the leg holes and twist the ends together. Draw the spider's face.

WHAT TO DO

- Follow steps one to four to makethe spiders' webs with the children.
- As you make the webs with the children, introduce mathematical language by asking them to count how many triangular shapes they can see. Tell them to notice how the web is a spiral shape with triangles radiating out from the centre. Ask them to count the legs on the spider.

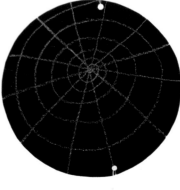

4 For the finishing touches, thread the elastic from the spider to the web. Tie a looped piece of elastic at the top of the web.

WHERE DO ANIMALS LIVE?

This chapter provides a range of informative activities to motivate children into thinking about where different animals live, looking at those that live above ground, under ground and under water. Children are encouraged to use observation skills and to learn from reference and story books. Some of the activities are based within the children's own environment, but others will prompt them to think about environments further away. How certain animals adapt to their habitats is also covered, with children participating in activities that develop their knowledge about, for example, hibernation.

Activities in this chapter

1
Piggy homes
Use a story book to stimulate children's interest in where different animals live

2
Barney and Fred
Children will develop their memory skills by learning this rhyme, and think more about how animals and humans differ from each other

3
Hibernating homes
Explore with children why some animals hibernate and what sort of places they choose

4
Wild bear's den
In this activity, children can use their imagination and think about what it would be like to be a hibernating bear

5
Under a stone
Children will love learning this rhyme and it will stimulate their interest in nature

6
Creepy crawlies
Take the children on a nature hunt as a follow-on activity to Under a Stone

7
Bird's nest
Show children how interesting reference books can be by combining information with a practical project

8
Animals that burrow
Use picture books to show children how some animals make their homes below ground

9
Counting fish
This rhyme will develop children's counting abilities and they will enjoy joining in the accompanying actions

10
Oceans
This activity will introduce children to the types of creatures that live in the oceans

1 Piggy homes

To develop an understanding of the differences between animals and humans

To enjoy listening to stories and to express throughts coherently

EXTENSION IDEA

Using junk, create a farmyard scene with pig sties, hen coops, cow sheds and so on.

Use the story, The Three Little Pigs, to discuss how animals do not live in homes like we do.

▶ WHAT TO DO

- Read the story to the children and ask them if they think all pigs live in houses. Explain that the pigs in the story are imaginary and that real pigs usually live on farms.
- Talk about the wolf in the story and ask the children where they think wolves live.
- Explain that some animals are domesticated and live on farms and that some animals are wild and live in the wild.

This activity works well as a follow on to a farm visit.

2 Barney and Fred

Materials and preparation

- wood shavings • hay
- bedclothes

To listen and respond to rhyme and begin to associate sounds with patterns in rhymes

To participate in group activities led by an adult

Questions

- What do the wood shavings and hay feel like?
- Do you think the hay would keep the guinea pig warm?
- Which other animals like to eat hay?

This entertaining rhyme highlights the differences between guinea pigs and humans.

Barney and Fred

Fancy eating your bed
Like the guinea pigs Barney and Fred
Who nibble away at
Wood shavings and hay.

I should never feel
Like making my house a meal
And gnawing the wood
To do my teeth good.

I never met anyone yet
Who ate the floor and carpet
Except, as I said
Barney and Fred.

Stanley Cook

▶ WHAT TO DO

- Recite the whole rhyme to the children then repeat two lines at a time.
- Ask the children to think about what is being said in each line.
- Show them the wood shavings, hay and bedclothes and ask them to compare the two kinds of bedding.

Hibernating homes

Materials and preparation
• A collection of soft toys that hibernate in winter a hedgehog, a bear, mouse etc.
• twigs • leaves • grass • brushwood

 To develop an understanding of different environments

 To learn to treat animals with care and respect

Contact the Hedgehog Preservation Society for information on how hedgehogs hibernate.

Hibernation is a subject that fascinates children but is often misunderstood.

▶ **WHAT TO DO**

• Explain that some animals hibernate during the cold winter months. Explain hibernation isn't the same as sleeping – during hibernation animals' metabolism is almost at a standstill, so they don't need to eat regularly to keep up their energy levels.
• Tell the children where small mammals hibernate – under hedges, in piles of leaves and so on.
• Show the children the twigs, leaves, grass and brushwood and the toy mice and hedgehogs. Let the children create warm environments in which the toy animals can hibernate.

4

Wild bear's den

Materials and preparation
• Brown sheet, children's paintings, cushions, soft bears, spot light,

 to use the den as a starting point for imaginative play

 To role play like a bear

 to play alongside other children.

Limit the number of children who go into in the bear cave so that it does not get too crowded.

This activity will encourage the children to pretend to be hibernating bears.

▶ **WHAT TO DO**

• Create the bear cave by tying two strings across the chosen corner. Throw over the brown sheet and decorate it with children's paintings. Put comfortable cushions inside and a spotlight in
• Read the children the song and story book We're Going on a Bear Hunt, by Rosen and Oxenbury, PUBL. Create a bear hunt dance around the nursery inside and outdoors.

Questions

• Why do you think bears hibernate in caves?
• What are caves like inside?
• Do you like the dark?
• Would you see a bear in this country?

5 Under a stone

To use their bodies expressively

To enjoy reciting rhymes and joining in with others

To listen attentively and memorise rhyme

This activity can be used in conjunction with the minibeast activities in chapter three.

Under a stone

Under a stone where the earth was firm,
I found a wiggly, wriggly worm;
(Use forefinger for the worm and cover with other hand)

'Good morning,' I said.
'How are you today?'
(Uncover the finger)

But the wiggly worm just wriggled away!
(Wriggle the forefinger up the other arm)

WHAT TO DO

- Teach the children the words and action to accompany the rhyme.
- Ask them what else they think may, likewise, live under a stone.
- Go outside, lift a stone and look at what is underneath it.

EXTENSION IDEAS

Invent a worm dance for the children, encouraging them to wriggle like worms. You could bring in percussion instruments, too, and allow children to provide a musical accompaniment to the worm dance.

Make sure the children wash their hands thoroughly after exploring in the garden.

---

6 Creepy crawlies

Materials and preparation
- Magnifying glasses

To explore and recognise the features of living things

To treat living things and their environment with care and concern

TIP • Tell the children that they must leave things as they found them and if they lift up stones they must put them back afterwards.

A nature hunt can be used as a follow on to 'Under a stone' (6) above.

WHAT TO DO

- Go out on a nature hunt.
- Give the children magnifying glasses to encourage their observation skills.
- Take photographs of the children doing their search so that you have a pictorial record.
- Back in the nursery, make a class book recording the different animals observed.

Questions

- Did things look smaller or larger than usual when looked at through a magnifying glass?
- Do you recognise any of the animals under the stones?

7   Birds' nest

Materials and preparation

- large circles of brown sugar paper
- blue paper • materials from a nature hunt • twigs • leaves • feathers
- shreds of paper • glue • scissors

To work with a variety of different materials

To understand and respect the natural world

Ensure the children do not pick up their picture until it is dry because otherwise they will lose all the parts of their nest.

1 Prepare a table with all the materials

R ead the children 'Eyewitness Bird' by David Burnie, Dorling Kindersley to show children what birds' nests are made of.

2 Glue all the materials that you think will create a good bird's nest on to the circle of card.

3 Once the nest is complete, cut out egg shapes from the blue paper and stick them in the nest.

▶ WHAT TO DO

- Use a reference book such as 'Eyewitness Bird' by David Burnie, Dorling Kindersley, to talk about birds' nests.
- Contact the Royal Society for the Protection of Birds and ask them for relevant information.
- Show the children an old birds' nest and dismantle it with them so that they can see how it was built and the materials used.
- Take the children on a nature trail and encourage them to collect items such as feathers and twigs.
- Let them build their own nests (see steps 1–3).

Questions

- Why do birds make nests?
- What materials do they use for their nests?
- What shape are they?
- Where would you find a bird's nest?

---

8   Animals that burrow

Materials and preparation

- reference books showing animals burrowing such as Let's all dig and burrow by A. Nilsen & A. Axworthy, Zero to Ten, and 'The Burrow Book', Dorling Kindersley

EXTENSION IDEAS

Encourage the children to draw cross-sections of animal burrows in different habitats. Annotate the drawings with their comments and make a wall display. Add toy animals to the habitats.

U se illustrated books to remind children that not all animals live above ground.

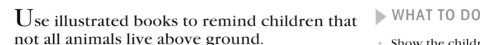

To work purposefully alongside other children

To enjoy books and handle them with care

To understand why animals burrow, and to think about manmade tunnels such as the Channel Tunnel

▶ WHAT TO DO

- Show the children the picture books and talk about the animals that live underground.
- Talk about the underground habitats and how they vary.
- Ask the children which animals keep warm/cool by burrowing.

9

Counting fish

To learn the words to a song

To enjoy singing and join in with others

To be able to perform actions to accompany a song

Questions

- Have you ever caught a fish yourself?
- Which is your right hand?
- Which is your left hand?

This is a song you can sing as a follow up to any of the activities in this chapter.

One, two, three, four, five,
(Count on fingers)

Once I caught a fish alive;
(Wriggle hand like a fish)

Six, seven, eight, nine, ten,
(Count on fingers)

Then I let him go again.
(Pretend to throw fish back)

Why did you let him go?
Because he bit my finger so!
(Shake hand violently)

Which finger did he bite?
This little finger on my right!
(Hold up little finger of right hand)

▶ **WHAT TO DO**

- Teach the children the words of the song. Then introduce the actions that are in brackets. Ask them the questions on the left.

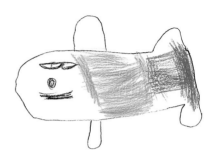

Oceans

Materials and preparation

- Books with ocean creatures such as 'Where am I?' by M. Butterfield and S. Calder, Belihtha Press, and 'Find and fit Ocean' by E. Bolam, Campbell Books • posters, stickers and so on of ocean scenes and animals • globe or world map showing the oceans • paints • paint brushes • paper • blue backing paper • blue and green crêpe paper • glue • scissors

To explore the properties of a range of art materials

To enjoy looking at reference books and understand that (in English) print runs from left to right

To develop an understanding of life in the ocean

EXTENSION IDEAS

- Repeat the same method for a different environment such as a river or a rain forest.
- Make a clay model of your favourite animal from the ocean.

Work together to make an ocean display.

1 Using books and posters for reference ask the children to paint their favourite ocean creatures.

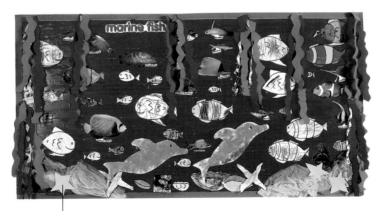

Add brightly coloured coral, starfish and other living things along the seabed.

▶ **WHAT TO DO**

- Show the children the reference material. Look through it together and talk about the huge variety of animals that live in water.
- Explain that oceans are huge areas of water that divide up the world and that they are very deep.
- Talk about the kinds of animal and plant that are found in oceans and how colourful they are.

2 Create a blue background to represent the ocean and use strips of green and blue crêpe paper to represent seaweed. Stick the children's paintings on to the background. Encourage the children to draw all kinds of sea creature, not just fish.

Supply fluorescent felt-tipped pens so that the children can emulate the colours of the ocean creatures in their drawings.

WILD ANIMALS

All the activities in this chapter help to develop children's understanding of the differences between wild animals and domestic pets. They encourage children to think about what different wild animals look like, the evidence they leave behind – such as hoof or paw prints – and how they behave. Children's knowledge of the natural world is broadened, too, as they consider the variety of habitats that wild animals live in and how they have adapted to their conditions – the polar bear's thick coat, for example. There are fun and informative art activities, and children will develop early literacy skills by writing invitations.

Activities in this chapter

1   What animal am I?

To speak clearly and listen when others are talking

To play along side other children and take turns with them. Can participate in a group activity led by an adult.

To move confidently and with increasing control when imitating animals

Give clues such as 'I've got four legs, black and white stripes and sometimes I run really fast' so that children learn about each animal.

▶ WHAT TO DO

- Ask the children to sit in a circle. Tell them you are going to pretend to be an animal and you will give them clues so that they can guess what you are.
- Repeat this activity several times, pretending you are a different wild animal.
- Ask the children in turn to pretend to be a wild animal. Tell the others to guess the animal.

👍 Repeat this activity several times so that children build up confidence to act in front of the group. Encourage very shy children by telling them what they are doing right.

---

2   Wild animal patterns

To work confidently with a variety of different materials

To be able to use a glue stick and scissors.

To use mathematical language to describe shape and colour

Questions

- What colours can you see in the fur?
- What does it feel like?
- Can you see a repeating pattern in the fur?
- Can you think of any wild animals that have fur like this?

This activity will encourage the children to look very carefully at the fur of wild animals.

1 Display some different examples of fake fabric fur so that the children can look at them and feel them.

2 Write out questions above the display. Tell the children that the fur is fake, not from real animals.

▶ WHAT TO DO

- Cover the board with fake fur fabrics. Encourage the children to look at them.
- Talk to the children about fur, describing the colours and patterns, such as stripes or spots. Display the children's pictures alongside the fur display.
- Tell the children to create their own fur pattern by cutting shapes out of coloured paper and gluing them on to another sheet.

👍 Ask parents and local fabric shops for any spare pieces or off-cuts of fake animal fur.

Rebecca

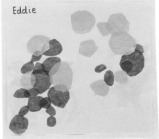

Eddie

3   Elmer the elephant

To encourage respect for individuals and animals

To recognise and name a range of colours

To listen to stories and respond with appropriate language

Questions

- Where does Elmer live?
- What colours can you see on Elmer?
- What do you notice about Elmer's pattern?
- How does Elmer make you feel?
- Do you know of any other colourful animals?
- Have you ever seen a patchwork elephant?

Elmer's patchwork looks make him different to other elephants. Using him for this activity encourages children to celebrate individuality.

Encourage the children to go to the library to see if they can find another Elmer story.

> **WHAT TO DO**

- Read 'Elmer' by David McKee, published by Red Fox, to the children and encourage them to look closely at the pictures.
- Ask the children some questions (see left).
- Talk about the ways in which Elmer is different from other elephants.
- Explain that real elephants are wild animals and talk about where children may see them.

4   What do elephants look like?

Materials and preparation

- pictures of elephants
- elephant models

To show respect and understanding for wild animals

To enjoy listening to stories and to enlarge their vocabulary

EXTENSION IDEAS

- Set up a display of elephant pictures and models to refer to.
- Use the information in the back of 'Little Elephant Thunderfoot' to teach children about conservation issues.
- Explain that elephants come from countries such as India and Africa. Show pictures of these places.

This activity is based on 'Little Elephant Thunderfoot' by Sally Grindley and John Butler, Orchard Books.

> **WHAT TO DO**

- Ask the children to gather in a circle then show them the book and the elephant models.
- As you read the story, discuss the elephant's body parts, such as its trunk with the children. Ask the children to point out the body parts on the elephant models.
- Each time you introduce new language take time to explain its meaning to the children and let them practise using new words appropriately.

5

Wild puppets

This project encourages children to think about what different animal faces look like.

Materials and preparation

selection of pictures showing animals' faces · paper bags · powder paints · paintbrushes

 To use paints to create a face

 To follow simple instructions
To work purposefully alongside other children

 To count and to name simple geometrical shapes

TIPS Introduce mathematical language by asking the children to count and describe the shapes of the animals' features. You could start the role play by singing the animal ark song on page 57.

- Show the children the animal face pictures. Explain that they are going to make animal face puppets to use as props in role play.
- Ask the children to paint animal faces on the paper bags. Encourage them to study the pictures closely for reference.

6

Wild card invitations

To extend Wild puppets (5) page 41, why not invite parents and friends to a puppet show?

Materials and preparation

A4 coloured card folded in half · crêpe paper · scissors · glue · animal stickers · white paper · pencils

 To be able to use scissors and apply stickers

 To use writing to convey meaning

Questions

Who are you going to invite to the show?
What message must an invitation have?
What animals are you sticking on to your invitation?
Which animals live in the trees and which animals live on the ground?

If you do not have any animal stickers, improvise by cutting out animals from greeting cards, magazines and wrapping paper to glue in place.

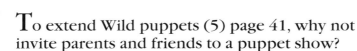

1 Help the children make an animal habitat on a folded card using crêpe paper and coloured card.

2 Encourage the children to think about where the animals live then give them the stickers to put on.

- Help the children to make the front of their card.
- Ask them who they would like to invite to the puppet show. Tell them to copy the invitation message on to white paper.

TIP If any of the children have difficulties copying the message, scribe it for them. Encourage them to practise making marks and then try writing the message in any way they wish. Let them draw a picture for the invitation, then complete the invitation for them.

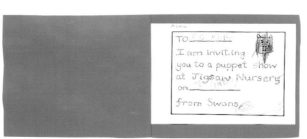

3 Stick each child's written message inside their card.

Materials and preparation

- potatoes · knife · paint or printing ink
- sugar paper · trays · pictures of animals

 To be able to print using a tool

 To work alongside other children and to respect their work

 To follow a trail

+ Tell the children to walk carefully on the trail of paper sheets so that they do not slip.

If possible, take children on an animal paw print hunt before running this activity.

1 An adult must cut the potatoes in half, then cut out a variety of simple animal foot prints such as paw or hoof shapes.

2 Spread four sheets of paper in front of each child. Tell them to make the prints as if the animal is walking across the paper.

3 Once the prints are dry, put them on the floor. Arrange the trail to lead to a picture of an animal. Ask the children to name the animal.

▶ WHAT TO DO

- Set up a large table so the children have enough space to spread out their paper to make a trail of animal paw prints.
- Encourage the children to esure that they have the correctamount of paint on their potatoes. This will be much easier if you put the paint in shallow trays lined with sponge. Show the children how to coat the potatoes with a thin, even layer of paint.
- Make sure the paintings are completely dry before using them to form a trail and asking the children to walk on them.

Questions

- Which animals do you think that these prints belong to?
- When do animals leave paw prints behind?
- Have you ever made your own foot prints?
- What do paw prints tell us about animals?

☀ EXTENSION IDEAS

- Show the children how to make prints in sand.
- Encourage them to make hand and foot prints in paint on paper. You could cut the hand prints out and display them in the toilet area to remind them to wash their hands.

TIP · After the children have made prints in paint, supervise hand and foot washing in a bowl of warm water. Do not let the children go anywhere before their hands and feet are washed or paint will be transferred to walls and floors.

8 Owl babies

To explore feelings and fears, and to develop understanding of wild birds

To listen attentively and respond to a story

Questions

Where do owls live?
Why were the owls frightened?
What do owls do?
Where do owls like to sit?
What does a mother owl hunt for so that she can feed her baby owls?

Listening to this story reminds children that many birds are wild and must hunt for food.

Show the children the pictures. Tell them how they relate to the story. Remember that the theme of fear and abandonment has powerful emotional relevance to them.

► WHAT TO DO

- Read 'Owl Babies' by Martin Waddell, Walker Books.
- Talk about where the owls live, and what they use to build their nests.
- Discuss the kinds of food they eat.
- Compare the differences between the owls' life style and that of people.

---

9 Fish in the sea

Materials and preparation

- blue and green tissue paper · glue
- glitter · blue A4 card · felt-tipped pens · scissors

To be able to talk about pictures. To be creative using a variety of materials

EXTENSION IDEAS

- Encourage the children to look through some sea-themed books to find out more about fish habitats.
- Create an underwater display with the pictures, adding long strips of crêpe paper and tissue paper.

Make sure the children work on a piece of paper so that glitter can be easily put back in the pot.

This activity encourages children to think about fish and their under-water world.

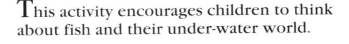

1 Show the children how to tear tissue paper and stick it in place. Apply glue then shake on glitter.

2 Draw the shape of a fish on the piece of card. Ask the children to decorate the fish with felt-tipped pens. Cut out the fish and stick it on to the sea environment.

► WHAT TO DO

- Explain to the children that many things live in water, such as plants, fish and sea creatures.
- Encourage the children to think about what water looks like. Show them how to glue strips of blue and green tissue paper on to a piece of paper in a random pattern that resembles water.
- Show them how to glue glitter on to paper to look like sparkling water.

Questions

- What do fish eat when they live in the sea?
- How do fish travel?
- Do you have you any fish as pets?
- How do fish breathe under water?
- What other sea creatures can you think of?

10 Crocodile rhyme

To listens and respond to rhymes

TIP • Read out the lines slowly so that the children can hear the rhyme. Say two lines at a time and ask the children to repeat them back to you. Repeat the rhyme regularly over several days so that the children start to remember it.

Use this rhyme to help children understand the importance of respecting wild animals and learn how they can be dangerous.

If you should meet a crocodile,
Don't take a stick and poke him;
Ignore the welcome in his smile,
Be careful not to stroke him!
For as he sleeps upon the Nile
He thinner gets and thinner;
So whenever you meet a crocodile
He's ready for his dinner

▶ WHAT TO DO

• Introduce the rhyme. Talk to the children about how it makes them feel. Pose questions such as: "Why are we careful of wild animals?" "Why do zoos keep wild animals?"

Questions

• Have you ever seen a crocodile?
• Which countries do you find crocodiles in?
• What do crocodiles eat?
• Where do crocodiles spend most of their time
• What do you think crocodile skin feels like?

11 Snappy crocks

Materials and preparation

• pictures of crocodiles for the children to refer to • hard-boiled eggs • crocodile template from page xx enlarged and drawn on to a piece of white A4 paper – one for each child • glue • paints • paintbrushes

To handle and use tools with increasing control

To use an everyday item in a different but purposeful way

TIP • The most effective way to obtain egg shells is by hard boiling the eggs. This way the shell is much easier to peel off. Also, the egg is not wasted because it can be eaten.

Encourage the children to look at nature books so that they can learn more about crocodiles and their natural habitat.

Now the children know how fierce crocodiles are they will be sure to enjoy making a snappy crock themselves.

1 Stick the pieces of egg shell on to the pre-drawn crocodile template with glue.

2 Allow the glue to dry then paint over the egg shell with green paint.

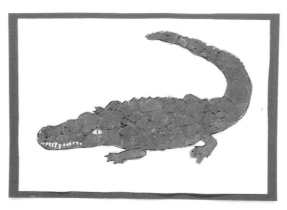

3 Add sharp white teeth and menacing eyes.

▶ WHAT TO DO

• Hard boil your eggs and break off their shells. Let the shells dry. Allow the children to crush the shells and stick the small pieces on to the crocodile template. Encourage the children to completely cover the crocodile, not leaving any spaces.
• Once the picture is dry, let the children paint it.

Questions

• What do you think a real crocodile skin feels like?
• How many teeth do you think a crocodile has?
• How do you think a crocodile moves?
• Do you think a crocodile prefers being in the water or on the land?

Percy stories

Materials and preparation

use props to help the children believe in the imaginary game – you could wear a hat like Percy the Park Keeper's for your role – think about what props could help the children create their animal roles – for example, a sheet for the fox and a balloon for the hedgehog

 To listen attentively to stories

 To use their imagination during role play activities

Take the children to the local library to find other animal story books on which to base role play.

P retend to be Percy the Park Keeper and encourage the children to develop their imaginations by acting the roles of the animals.

As Percy plodded on he saw his friend the fox coming up the path towards him. The fox was on his way home too.

"Good night," said Percy as they passed each other. "Good night, hic-Percy," answered the fox. The fox had hiccups.

▶ WHAT TO DO

- Choose a story to read from 'Tales from Percy's Park' by Nick Butterworth, Collins.
- After reading the story, ask the children to choose roles and act out the story with them.

Questions

- Ask questions that will encourage the children to get into their role: Hello foxy, how are you? What shall we do in the park today foxy?
- Make sure that each child has a turn acting a role.

---

13   Giraffe measure

Materials and preparation

pictures and drawings of a wide variety of wild animals • a range of wild animal models of varying sizes • giraffe collage, about 6ft high, fixed to the wall to measure the children's heights against

To see that creative projects can be done on a large scale

To develop an understanding of concepts such as taller/shorter and bigger/smaller

This activity uses large and small wild animals to develop mathematical language.

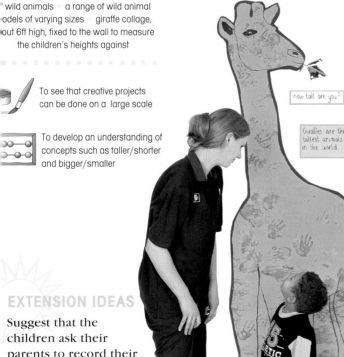

how tall are you?

Giraffes are the tallest animals in the world

TIP • To make the giraffe collage, cut out a giraffe shape from a roll of orange paper. Cut out shapes from different-coloured pieces of paper to represent the giraffe's patch markings.

EXTENSION IDEAS

Suggest that the children ask their parents to record their heights at home so they can see how much they grow in a year, and how tall they are compared to their brothers and sisters.

▶ WHAT TO DO

- Show the children the wild animal pictures. Talk about the relative sizes of the animals.
- Let the children have fun putting the animal models in order from the smallest to the largest.
- Talk to them about the differences between a large animal and a tall animal, and a small animal and a short one.
- Explain that giraffes are the tallest animals and show them the measure. This should be the height of a tall adult (about 2 metres/6 feet). Before this activity, plan the best place to put the measure in the room.
- Measure each of the children in turn and write their names next to the mark that represents their height.

Add long grass around the giraffe's feet to remind children of its habitat.

ANIMALS OF THE WORLD

The activities in this chapter focus on encouraging children to become interested in animals they may not have previously experienced, and the different environments in which they live. By introducing the children to concepts such as hot and cold conditions they will be able to understand more about the animals that live in, say, the tropical rainforest or the freezing arctic. In addition to a greater understanding of the world's animals, the activities also develop in a variety of fun and imaginative ways the children's literacy, creativity, memory and organisational and observational skills.

Activities in this chapter

1
Let's go to the zoo
Children will enjoy joining in with this song and will feel enthusiastic about an informative trip to the zoo

2
Rainforest bird jigsaw
In this activity children will develop observational and constructive skills, and gain an interest in the rainforest and the creatures that live there

3
Jungle Stories
These stories will encourage children to be able to hear rhyme and develop an interest in words

4
World animal game
Children will enjoy playing this game, that encourages visual skills and concentration

5
Polar bears
In this activity children are encouraged to think about the features animals have that allow them to survive in their habitats

6
It's freezing
Children will be fascinated to see how a liquid can be transformed into a solid

7
Hot and cold
In this activity children find out how to organise pictures into categories while learning more about animals, too

8
Desert scene
This practical activity gives children knowledge about what life is like for animals in the desert

9
Where animals live
Children will enjoy creating a model representing the arctic and will think about what this habitat would be like to live in

Let's go to the zoo

To listen and respond to songs

Can join in a group activity led by an adult.

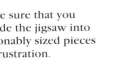
The words for subsequent verses can be found in Apusskidu A&C Black

This song is a fun introduction to a zoo visit, which is an invaluable learning experience.

Going to the Zoo

Dad - dy's tak-ing us to the zoo to - mor - row

zoo to - mor - row zoo to - mor - row

Dad - dy's tak-ing us to the zoo to - mor - row

We can stay all day. We're go - ing to the

Zoo, zoo, zoo. How a - bout

You, you, you? You can come too, too,

too, we're go - ing to the zoo, zoo, zoo.

EXTENSION IDEAS

Cut out pictures of zoo animals from magazines. Ask children to sort the animals into groups such as scaly-skinned reptiles, big cats and so on.
Ask all the children to draw a picture of their favourite zoo animal.

▶ WHAT TO DO

- Teach the children this rhyme as an introduction to a zoo visit. Repeat the lines until the children have memorized them.
- Ask the children which is their favourite zoo animal.
- Ask them which zoo animal they think is the largest.
- Which is the fiercest?

Questions

- Which different animals do you think you will find in the zoo?
- Why do some animals live in zoos?
- Can you think of habitats where different zoo animals might live?

2

Rainforest bird jigsaw

Materials and preparation

· magazines with pictures of rain forest animals · scissors · black felt-tipped pen · laminating machine or sticky backed plastic

To enjoy joining in an activity with an adult

To use a pair of scissors appropriately

To count jigsaw pieces and recreate a jigsaw

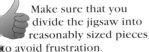
Make sure that you divide the jigsaw into reasonably sized pieces to avoid frustration.

Making a jigsaw develops constructive skills and encourages an interest in the rainforest.

1 Choose a picture, preferably of a rainforest animal or bird, from a magazine. On the chosen picture an adult must outline the jigsaw pieces.

2 There should be more pieces for very able children and fewer for younger children. Ask the child to cut out the pieces.

▶ WHAT TO DO

- Help the child to select a picture. Draw the jigsaw outline over the picture then laminate it. Ask the child to cut out the pieces. Mix up the pieces. Help the child to reconstruct the picture. The child can then share it with a friend.

Questions

- Which animal or bird is on your jigsaw?
- How many pieces are in your jigsaw?
- Do you have any other jigsaws at home?
- How long does it take for you to complete your jigsaw?

3 Jungle stories

Materials and preparation

- 'Safari Animals' by Paul Hess, Zero to ten • 'Rumble in the Jungle' by Giles Andreae and David Wojtowycz, Orchard books • note paper

Y our children will soon be rumbling in the jungle and interacting with the text of these wonderful stories.

Ask the children to make up their own rhyming sentences.

To be able to hear rhyme and offer the word that is missing from the text

▸ WHAT TO DO

- Read both the stories to the children at the beginning of the session
- At the end of the session re-read the stories, covering up the rhyming words with your hand.
- As you read the children will then have to predict the missing rhyming word. For example, 'It's great to be a chimpanzee swinging through the trees. And if we can't find nut to eat we munch each others ...'

4 World animal game

Materials and preparation

- for four children, photocopy the template on p.62 six times • paper • piece of card or baseboard • scissors • sticky-backed plastic • cube to act as dice • coloured pencils

To match using two attributes

To take turns and understand rules

T his activity will encourage the children to talk about animals from all over the world.

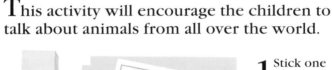

1 Stick one photocopied template sheet onto the baseboard. Cut up the remaining templates. Stick one set on each side of a cube. The rest form playing cards.

Game rules

- Each child is given one set of picture cards.
- The children take turns to roll the 'dice' covered with animal pictures.
- Children match their picture cards to the animal that is face up on the rolled dice by placing their relevant card on the baseboard.
- If the child has previously placed that picture card, they do not place a card but pass the dice on to the next player.

2 Cover the baseboard and playing cards with sticky backed plastic for extra durability.

3 Give each child one set of cards and follow the game rules on the right.

TIP Trace the animal templates onto coloured paper so that younger children can match the colours rather than the more complex animal pictures.

5   Polar animals

To participates and contribute in a group activity

To listens and respect others.

EXTENSION IDEAS

- Ask the children to draw the different clothes they like to wear in hot and cold weather.
- Now tell the children to draw hot and cold foods.

Encourage children to consider where polar animals live and why they have thick coats.

👍 Provide lots of adult clothes so that all the children can put them over what they are wearing and feel they are dressed up for their polar animal roles.

▶ WHAT TO DO

- Ask the children to form a circle. Read 'Polar Animals' to the children. Make sure that they look closely at the different animal pictures.
- Put a huge pile of clothes in the middle of the circle. Request that one child volunteers to dress up like a polar animal. What will he or she need to protect themselves from an icy habitat?.

Questions

- Where do polar animals live?
- Why do polar animals have such thick coats?
- What activities do you do in the cold?
- When do you usually wear warm clothes?

6   It's freezing

To watch something change over a period of time.

To develop observational skills.

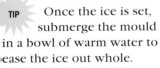

TIP Once the ice is set, submerge the mould in a bowl of warm water to ease the ice out whole.

EXTENSION IDEA

In summer, make fresh fruit juice ice cubes.

This is a wonderful way for children to observe liquid changing to a solid.

▶ WHAT TO DO

- Show the children that you are filling the mould with water and a few drops of food dye.
- Put the mould inside a freezer and leave until the water is frozen. Remove the ice fish from the mould and place in a deep tray for the children to observe and touch.

Questions

- What has the water turned into?
- How does the fish feel when you touch it?
- What do you think the ice will turn into?
- When do you see ice?

7

Hot and cold

Materials and preparation

• animal pictures from magazines
• scissors • squares of card • glue
• sticky-backed plastic • two pieces of
card or paper labelled 'Hot' and 'Cold'

EXTENSION IDEAS

• Encourage the children to talk about their decisions, such as by explaining why a polar bear has a cold habitat.
• Ask the children to collect the pictures and sort them by colour. They can continue to categorise by sorting animals into those with and without legs.

Sorting animals of the world into different categories promotes discussion about them.

  To talk freely to other children and adults

  To develop knowledge of habitats and how animals adapt to them

To sort by one attribute

Make sure you have a reasonable amount of animals for each category.

▶ WHAT TO DO

• Ask the children to cut out pictures of animals from magazines. Cut out card squares for them to stick the pictures on to. Put on sticky-back plastic
• Lay out the two titles, 'Hot' and 'Cold'. Place the pictures in front of the children and ask them to sort the animals into categories.

Questions

• Name the animals that have cold habitats
• Name the animals that have hot habitats.
• What do you notice about the animals that have cold habitats?
• What do you notice about animals with hot habitats?

Desert scene

Materials and preparation

• sandpit • foil • brown card • green paper • scissors • clear sticky tape
• plastic model camels, snakes, palms, cacti and other desert artefacts

 To play purposely on own or with a partner

 To gain an understanding of how paper can be used creatively

 To explore the properties of sand when wet and dry

Pour a little water on to the sand and show the children how they can mould the sand into dunes and so on.

Use this sandpit activity to introduce the idea of what life is like for animals in the desert.

▶ WHAT TO DO

• Encourage the children to help to turn the sandpit into a desert scene.
• Cut out a circle of foil for the oasis. Make palm trees by rolling card into a tube and securing the edges with sticky tape. Cut out strips of crêpe paper for the palm leaves and stick them to the tube
• Let the children add the model camels, snakes and other desert items.

Questions

• Which animals live in the desert?
• What is the weather like in the desert?
• Where do animals drink in the desert?
• Which countries have desert habitats?

Animal habitats

Materials and preparation

range of art materials to make chosen animal habitats · model animals native to a variety of habitats · range of reference, story and picture books depicting animals in a range of habitats – see booklist on page xx

To speak clearly and listen when others are speaking.

To learn about a range of environments and animal habitats

To sort according to set criteria

To describe features of living things and select appropriate materials

These activities will encourage children to learn about a wide range of animal habitats throughout the world.

1 Animals in the arctic could include polar bears, penguins, seals, arctic foxes, reindeer and walruses.

▶ WHAT TO DO

- Make a three-dimensional polar habitat with the children. Show it to them and ask which animals they think live at the poles. Make sure they realise that different animals live at the north and south poles.
- Look at the picture books and ask the children to describe the polar animals. Talk about how they have adapted to their cold environment with warm coats and layers of fat.
- With reference material, talk about other habitats.

Questions

- Which animals do you think live in the arctic and antartic?
- What is the weather like in the arctic and antartic?

2 To learn about safari animals, you could cut out safari views and animals from magazines or make colour copies from picture books. Laminate the images with sticky-backed plastic. Mount the scenes on to card. Glue Velcro squares on to the scenes and the animals. Let the children fix the animals in position.

TIP · Make sure that you find a complete box with all its flaps. Place the arctic scene at child's height and make sure that there are no obstacles to obstruct children's view.

Reinforce the lessons the children learn from the activity by prompting them with questions about the ways in which animals are adapted to their habitats.

3 To reinforce children's knowledge of all the animal habitats explored, make or buy a felt collage that shows a range of animal habitats. Attach felt animals with Velcro. Ask children to identify the correct habitat for each animal, then fix the animal in place.

ANIMAL WELFARE

This chapter is packed with activities that will encourage children to be responsible and acquire a caring attitude towards animals. To help them to develop respect for animals, there is an activity that looks at the valuable roles performed by working animals, such as police horses and guide dogs. The important issues of conservation and extinction are also covered, so that children can understand how animals need specific habitats to survive. There are many creative activities, too, that both reinforce the information and allow children to feel that they can do something to help endangered animals.

Activities in this chapter

1
Caring for cats
In this activity children are encouraged to care for domestic pets and to understand their needs

2
Bird feeders
Children will learn constructional skills in this activity, while becoming aware of how wildlife may suffer in winter unless they lend a helping hand

3
Hedgehog awareness
In this activity, children find out how and why some animals hibernate during the winter months

4
Working animals
This activity develops children's understanding of how animals can be trained to help people in a variety of ways

5
My Dog
Encourage children to think, and share with each other, their own experiences of how dogs behave

6
Conservation
Reading the children this story will develop their awareness of the plight of animals around the world and the necessity for their habitats to be preserved

7
Bears of the world
Show children pictures of the different types of bears that live around the world and show them how to make a 'Save the Bear' poster

8
Panda painting
In this activity children will develop their observational skills and gain a concern for the fascinating animals that are in danger of extinction

9
Animal ark song
Children will enjoy learning the words of a song that encourages them to think about all the different animals that went into the ark

1   Caring for cats

Materials and preparation

· grass seed (obtainable from most pet shops) · tub · soil or compost · watering can · soft toy cat.

 To enjoy watching something grow and change.

 To observe growth and change in living things

Questions

· Why do cats eat grass?
· Why do people choose to care for cats?
· Do you have a cat?

Teach children the need to care for pet cats, using this project as an ideal starting point.

1 Scatter the grass seed over a tub of soil or compost. Rake it in lightly with your fingers.

2 Water the seed regularly. Tell the children to notice the grass growing. This may take up to 14 days but it will germinate within a few days in a warm place.

▶ WHAT TO DO

· Talk to the children about why cats eat grass. Cats are clean animals and spend many hours grooming themselves. This sometimes means they get fur in their tummies. Eating grass is important for cats as it helps them to bring up the fur and makes them feel a lot better.

---

2   Bird feeders

Materials and preparation

Contact the RSPB for advice, information and posters · Reference books on identifying bird species · coconut · knife or sharp implement · spoon · string · bird seed · lard

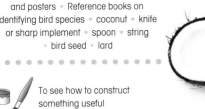 To see how to construct something useful

 To go out into the local environment and help hang up the bird feeder

TIP · Once your feeders are hanging in a tree, tell the children to make regular observations of the variety of birds that visit them. Tell them that they must observe from a reasonable distance.

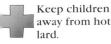 Keep children away from hot lard.

By helping to construct a bird feeder, children develop an awareness of wildlife.

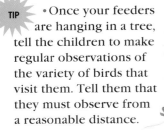

1 Cut the coconut in half so that a child can scoop out the flesh with a spoon. An adult must make holes in the top of the shell.

2 Show the children how to thread string through the holes, making sure the string is long enough to hang in a tree.

3 Showing the children, melt some lard and mix in bird seed. Pour the mixture into the feeder. When it is hard, hang up the feeder.

▶ WHAT TO DO

· An adult must first cut a coconut in half. Then a child can scoop out the flesh with a spoon. An adult makes two small holes in the top with a knife or sharp implement, as the shells can be tough.
· Once the children have threaded string through the holes, prepare the bird food for the feeder.

Questions

· What do birds like to eat?
· Why do we have to help birds find food?
· Can you name different types of birds?

Cutting the coconut in half makes two feeders so prepare enough nuts and lard to fill both. When one runs out you will have another.

Hedgehog awareness

Materials and preparation

• information pack from the British Hedgehog Preservation Society
• sugar • paper • twigs • leaves • sponges • powder paints

Questions

• Why do you think that hedehogs hibernate?
• Have you ever seen a hedgehog?
• Do you know any other animals that hibernate?
• When are hedgehogs at their most active?
• What habitats do hedgehogs live in?
• Why do hedgehogs have prickly spikes?

This activity can be used as an extension to Hibernating homes (3) page 34.

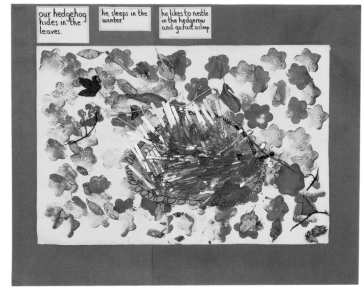

 To explore the reasons that some wild animals hibernate

 To work with natural materials

 To listen and respond to information being conveyed by an adult

▶ WHAT TO DO

• Tell the children about where hedgehogs like to hibernate – in bushes, leaves and so on.
• Talk about the time of year that hedgehogs hibernate and why they choose this time.
• Display illustrated material for the children to look at while you tell them about hedgehogs.
• Encourage the children to make a picture of a hedgehog using twigs. Then show them how to print the hedgehogs home – its hibinacula – using a sponge dipped in paint.

👍 Gather information on all aspects of hedgehogs – their habitat, diet, nocturnal activities and hibernation period.

Working animals

Materials and preparation

• pictures of a variety of working animals such as guide dogs, sheep dogs, police horses, sniffer dogs

 To join in group discussions lead by an adult

 To join in with question and answer sessions

Looking at different working animals introduces children to animals that help us.

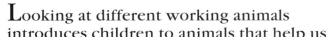

👍 Look in newspapers and magazines for pictures of various working animals.

EXTENSION IDEAS

Contact your local guide dog for the blind representative and ask if he or she would come in to talk to the children. Check whether it is possible for them to bring in a guide dog, too.

TIP • Explain that police horses go through special training so that they do not become frightened when in the middle of a crowd of people or when someone waves their arms about.

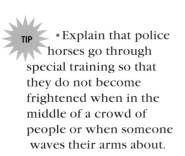

▶ WHAT TO DO

• Discuss the different types of animals children have learnt about – pets, domestic animals, wild animals. Explain that some animals are specially trained to help us in different ways.
• Talk about the variety of animal that fit into this category, including sheep dogs, police horses and guide dogs.
• Explain how each animal helps us – for example, sheep dogs herding sheep, police horses carrying police officers, guide dogs leading blind people.
• Talk about the needs of each working animal and explain why we must not treat them like pets.

My dog

Materials and preparation
'My Dog' by Jonathan Allen, MacMillan Children's Books

Ask an adult with a docile dog to bring it into the nursery to visit the children

She is very friendly and jumps up at everyone.

Some people don't like dogs and get a bit frightened.

 To be introduced to speach and thought bubbles

 To develop a caring attitude toward animals

This activity can be used as a follow on to Approaching pets (4) page 14.

▶ WHAT TO DO

- Read 'My Dog' by Johnathan Allen, Macmillan Children's Books.
- Tell the children to look at the pictures closely. Show them the speech bubbles and encourage them to imagine what the dog is thinking.
- Arrange for a docile dog to come into the nursery.

Questions

- Why is the dog put on a lead before going out?
- Are you or do you know anyone who is afraid of dogs?
- What do you have to do to care for a dog?
- How can you tell when a dog is happy or sad?

6

Saving the rainforest

Materials and preparation
'Where the forest meets the sea' by Jeannie Baker, Walker Books

 To listen to stories and join in with group activities

 To be aware of environments other than our own

This activity is based on 'Where the forest meets the sea' by Jeannie Baker, Walker Books.

Give the children plenty of time to look at the pictures so that they can see all the wonderful detail.

▶ WHAT TO DO

- Read the story and talk about each animal that lives in the rainforest.
- Ask the questions on the left and encourage the children to talk about the feelings they have on conservation.
- Ask the children how many different animals of the rainforest they can remember.

Questions
What animals can you see?
Why are some animals fading?
Will the forest still be here when we get back?
How does this story make you feel?

7   Bears around the world

Materials and preparation

- 'Bears of the World' poster and other relevant information from the World Society for the Protection of Animals
- different-coloured sugar paper and tissue paper • felt-tipped pens

👍 Put the poster up in a prominent place, so other children can ask questions about it.

Base this activity on information from World Society for the Protection of Animals.

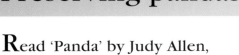
To use language to convey meaning

To use different materials for creative purposes

▶ WHAT TO DO

- Show the children the poster and talk to them about the different kinds of bears and where they live. Explain that, if these habitats are destroyed, there is a danger that some bear species could become extinct.
- Help the children to make their own 'Save the Bear' poster.

Questions

- What type of habitat does a polar bear live in?
- What other types of bears are there?
- Do they look different from polar bears?
- What type of habitats do other bears live in?

---

8   Preserving pandas

Materials and preparation

- 'Panda' by Judy Allen, Walker Books
- contact the World Wide Fund for Nature to request informative leaflets and posters • black and white paint
- paper • green tissue paper • scissors
- glue • bamboo shoots

To learn about and respect animals

To share points of view and engage in discussion

☀ EXTENSION IDEA

- Mount a display of information from the World Wide Fund for Nature. Show the children pictures of the habitat that pandas live in. Give them the positive news that pandas are being bred in zoos.

Read 'Panda' by Judy Allen, Walker Books, as a follow-on activity to Bears of the World.

1 Read the story to the children in clear language that they can understand. Give them plenty of opportunities to ask questions.

2 To reinforce the children's learning, ask them to make panda collages and stick on bamboo shoots.

▶ WHAT TO DO

- Show the children the book so that they can paint a panda picture.
- Explain that, unlike us, pandas can only eat one kind of food – bamboo shoots. Tell them bamboo is being cut down faster than it can grow – this is why pandas are in danger

👍 As a nursery, join the World Wide Fund for Nature. See page 59 for the address.

9 Animal ark song

Materials and preparation

• A Noah's ark and plastic toys • words of song and music • collection of plastic toy animals (make sure this includes animals from all around the world)

To do accompanying actions when singing

To listen and respond to songs

To enjoy singing and join in with others

To sort by kind and number

TIP As the children become confident with the song, introduce percussion instruments that some of the children can play to accompany it.

Questions

• How many animals went into the ark?
• Which is your favourite animal?
• What were the different animals called that went into the ark?

This popular song is ideal for talking about the different animals that went into the ark.

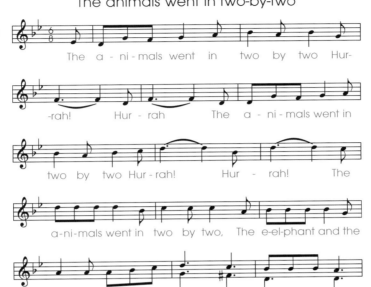

The animals went in two-by-two

The a-ni-mals went in two by two Hur-rah! Hur-rah The a-ni-mals went in two by two Hur-rah! Hur-rah! The a-ni-mals went in two by two, The e-el-phant and the kan-ga-roo, And they all went in-to the ark for to get out of the rain.

Use toy animals to reinforce children's mathematical development and to help them understand more about animals.

1 Place a collection of plastic toy animals in front of the children. Ask them to organize the toy animals into pairs with the same two animals together.

2 Now ask them to group the animals into threes, fours, and so on. Talk to the children about similarities and differences between types of animals, such as in colour and fur markings.

▶ WHAT TO DO

• Introduce the song to the children making up simple hand actions to accompany the words. Perhaps choose some children to stand up and be certain animals so that they can all see what two by two looks like.
• Put out an ark and some animals for the children to play with. Encourage the children to sing the song and pair the animals as they play.

Additional verses to this song can be found in 'Apusskidu' A&C Black.

Share 'Noah's Ark' by Lucy Cousins, Walker Books with the children, too.

Make sure that you have gathered together at least two of each type of toy animal before giving them to the children to organize.

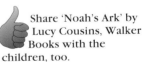

Resources

The resources section provides a useful range of material to supplement the activities in this book. The booklist below contains a selection of stories, information books, poems, and songs, and page 59 lists useful organisations to contact when planning a theme around animals. You will find templates for many of the creative activities on pages 60–63 and the index on page 64 lists every activity contained in **All About Animals**.

STORY BOOKS

'Bringing the Rain to Kapiti Plain', Verna Aardema. Macmillan.

'Dinosaurs Roar', Paul and Henrietta Stickland. Puffin.

'Dear Zoo', Rod Campbell. Picture Puffin.

'Elmer', David McKee. Red Fox.

'Farm Animals', Gallimard Jeunesse. Moonlight Publishing.

'Farmyard Animals', Paul Hess. Zero to ten.

'Goodnight Owl', Pat Hutchins. Puffin.

'Guess How Much I Love You' Sam McBratney. Walker Books.

'I Don't Want to Have a Bath', Julie Sykes. Magi Publications.

'It Was Jake', Anita Jeram. Walker Books.

'Kipper', Mick Inkpen. Picture Knight/Hodder.

'Let's Go Home Little Bear', Martin Waddell, Barbara Firth. Walker Books.

'Little Elephant Thunderfoot', Sally Grindley and John Butler. Orchard Books.

'My Dog', Jonathan Allen. Macmillan Children's Books.

'My Friend Whale', Simon James. Walker Books.

'Mr Gumpy's Motor Car', John Burningham. Puffin.

'Noah's Ark', Lucy Cousins. Walker Books.

'Oi! Get Off Our Train', John Burningham. Red Fox.

'Old Bear', Jane Hissey. Hutchinson.

'Owl Babies', Martin Waddell. Walker Books.

'Panda', Judy Allen. Walker Books.

'Penguin Small', Mick Inkpen. Hodder.

'Polar Animals', Paul Hess. Zero to ten.

'Rainforest Animals', Paul Hess. Zero to ten.

'Rainforest', Helen Cowcher. Picture Corgi.

'Rumble in the Jungle',Giles Andreae and David Wojitowycz. Orchard Books.

'Safari Animals', Paul Hess. Zero to ten.

'Spot' lift-the-flap books, Eric Hill. Penguin

'Tales from Percy's Park', Nick Butterworth. Collins.

'The Very Hungry Caterpillar', Eric Carle. Picture Puffin.

'The Prickly Hedgehog', Mark Azra. Magi Publications.

'The Pig in the Pond', Martin Waddell. Walker Books.

'The Rainbow Fish', Marcus Pfister. North South Books.

'The is the Bear', Sarah Hayes, Helen Craig. Walker Books

'The Park in the Dark', Martin Waddell, Barbara Firth. Walker Books.

'Wag Wag Wag', Peter Hansard. Walker Books.

'We're Going on a Bear Hunt', Michael Rosen, Helen Oxenbury. Walker Books.

'Where the Forest Meets the Sea', Jeannie Baker. Walker Books.

'Where the Wild Things Are', Maurice Sendak. Harper Collins.

INFORMATION BOOKS

'Amazing Animal Facts', Christopher Maynard. Dorling Kindersley.

'A Piece of Cake', Jill Murphy. Walker Books.

'Baby Animals', 'Farm Animals', 'Jungle Animals', 'Minibeasts', 'Night-time Animals', 'Pets', 'Sea Animals', 'Zoo Animals', are all in the DK Eye openers series. Dorling Kindersley.

'Birds', 'Butterflies', 'Cats', 'Dogs', 'Horses and Ponies', 'Insects' are all in Spotter's Sticker Books. Usbourne.

'Birds', 'Wild Animals', are both in the First Nature series. Usbourne.

'Egg', Jane Burton and Kim Taylor. Dorling Kindersley.

'Eyewitness Bird', David Burnie. Dorling Kindersley.

'Farm Animals' Duchess of Devonshire. Kyle Cathie Limited.

Resources

'Farmyard Animals', Paul Hess. Zero to Ten.
'Find and Fit Ocean', E. Bolam. Campbell Bools.
'How to look after your pet' series. Dorling Kindersley.
'Let's All Dig and Burrow', A. Nilsen and A. Axworthy. Zero to Ten.
'Let's Look at Baby Animals', Ladybird.
'The Big Book of Animals'. Dorling Kindersley.
'The Little Red Hen', Alan Garner. Dorling Kindersley.
'My Best Book of Creepy Crawlies', Claire Llewellyn. Kingfisher.
'Night-time Animals', (video). Dorling Kindersley.
'Polar Animals', Norman Barrett. Picture Library.
'The Burrow Book', Richard Orr. Dorling Kindersley.
'See How They Grow' video series on wildlife, narrated by Johnny Morris. Dorling Kindersley.
'The Really Amazing Animal Book'. Dorling Kindersley.
'The Very Busy Spider', Eric Carle. Penguin.
'Wild Animal Go-Round', Mary Ling. Dorling Kindersley.
'When I grow up', Steve Weatherill. Frances Lincoln.
'Where am I?', M. Butterfield and S. Calder. Belitha Press.

'Who's on the farm?', Naomi Russell. Walker Books.

POETRY, RHYMES AND MUSIC
'Animals Like Us', chosen by Tony Bradman. Puffin Books.
'Earthways Poems on Conservation Earthwise', selected by Judith Nicholls. Oxford University Press.
'Dragon Poems', John Foster. Oxford University Press.
'Owls and Pussy Cats Nonsense Verse', Edward Lear, Lewis Carroll. Oxford University Press.

The following books contain a range of useful poems, rhymes and music:
'Apusskidu'. A & C Black
'The Hutchinson Treasury of Children's Poetry', edited by Alison Sage. Hutchinson.
'The Jungle Cup Final and Other Poems', Richard Digance. Puffin.
'The New Oxford Treasury of Children's Poems. Oxford University Press.
'Nursery Rhymes'. Ladybird.
'This Little Puffin...' Puffin Books.

· ·

USEFUL ORGANISATIONS

Bat Conservation Trust
The Conservation Foundation
1 Kensington Gore
London SW7 2AR

British Hedgehog Preservation Society
Knowbury House
Knowbury, Ludlow
Shropshire SY8 3LQ

The Cats Protection League
17 Kings Road
Horsham
West Sussex, RH13 5PN

Guide Dogs for the Blind
Hillfields
Burghfield, Reading
Berkshire, RG7 3YG

National Canine Defence League
17 Wakley Street
London, EC1V 7LT

Royal Society for the Protection of Birds
The Lodge, Sandy
Bedfordshire SG17 2DL

RSPCA
Causeway, Horsham
West Sussex, RH12 1HG

World Society for the Protection of Animals
Education Department
2 Langley Lane
London, SW8 1TJ

World Wide Fund for Nature (WWF)
Panda House
Weyside Park
Godalming, GU7 1XR

We liked the colours and ticklish feeling of the feathers we glued to our peacocks tail.

Templates

BODY

WING CASES

Cut along dotted line

Ladybird template for Flying ladybirds (2) page 27.

Photocopy the template this size, cut out the body and legs in black card and the wing cases in red card.

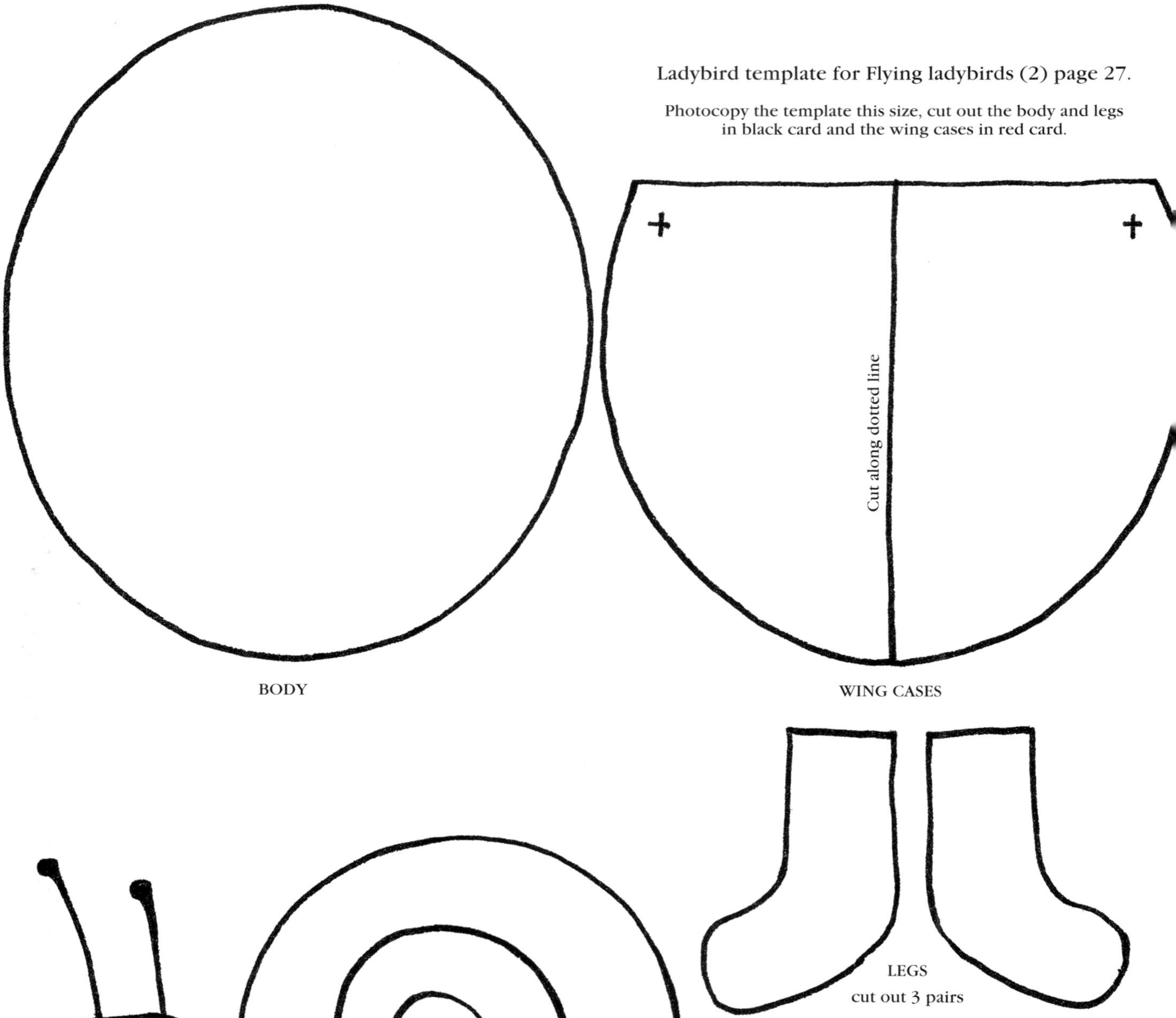

LEGS

cut out 3 pairs

Snail template for Snail spirals (8) page 30
Photocopy the snail to fill a page, extend trail to page edge.

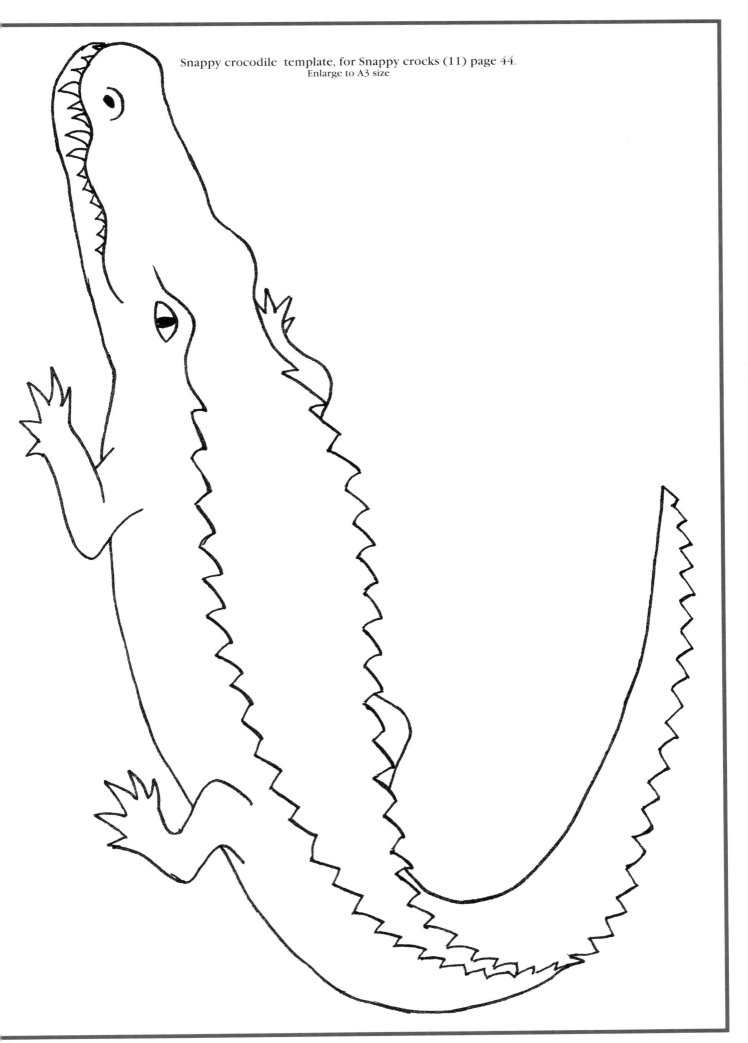

Snappy crocodile template, for Snappy crocks (11) page 44.
Enlarge to A3 size

Notes

Note down additional resources on this page.

Index

Acknowledgments

Nursery World would like to thank:

Hope Education for providing many of the props used in this book; Clare Shedden for props and templates; Alternative View Studios for Digital music; Colin Bunner for Digital artwork; Denise Blake for picture research; Little Folks Mobile Farm, Holly Dene, Bower Heath, Harpenden AL5 5EE; Standalone Farm, Wilbury Road, Letchworth Garden City, Herts SG6 4JN.

Picture credits:

T top; B bottom; C centre; L left; R right

Martyn Chillmaid/Oxford Scientific Films, 54BL; Nigel French/Collections 54BR; Sandi Friend 35BC, Maya Kardum 6TC, 15T, 15CL, 15CR; music ©1965 "Going to the Zoo" by Tom Paxton, Harmony Music Ltd., 11 Uxbridge Street, London W8 7TQ.

Every effort has been made to trace the copyright holders. Times Supplements apologises for any unintentional omissions and would be pleased, in such cases, to add an acknowledgment in future editions.